I0881643

The Legat Legacy

UNIVERSITY PRESS OF FLORIDA

Florida A&M University, Tallahassee
Florida Atlantic University, Boca Raton
Florida Gulf Coast University, Ft. Myers
Florida International University, Miami
Florida State University, Tallahassee
New College of Florida, Sarasota
University of Central Florida, Orlando
University of Florida, Gainesville
University of North Florida, Jacksonville
University of South Florida, Tampa
University of West Florida, Pensacola

THE LEGAT LEGACY

EDITED BY MINDY ALOFF

Foreword by Tasha Bertram
Introduction by Robert Greskovic

University Press of Florida
Gainesville / Tallahassee / Tampa / Boca Raton
Pensacola / Orlando / Miami / Jacksonville / Ft. Myers / Sarasota

Frontispiece: Nicolas Legat in *Paquita*, from *Heritage of a Ballet Master: Nicolas Legat*

Published in the United States of America

25 24 23 22 21 20   6 5 4 3 2 1

ISBN 978-0-8130-6812-1
Library of Congress Control Number: 2019950689

Originally published as *Ballet Russe: Memoirs of Nicolas Legat*, translated by Sir John Dukes, Methuen and Co., 1939, and *Heritage of a Ballet Master: Nicolas Legat*, compiled and edited by John Gregory in collaboration with André Eglevsky, Dance Horizons, 1977. Reprinted by permission of the trustees for the Legat Foundation.

The University Press of Florida is the scholarly publishing agency for the State University System of Florida, comprising Florida A&M University, Florida Atlantic University, Florida Gulf Coast University, Florida International University, Florida State University, New College of Florida, University of Central Florida, University of Florida, University of North Florida, University of South Florida, and University of West Florida.

University Press of Florida
2046 NE Waldo Road
Suite 2100
Gainesville, FL 32609
http://upress.ufl.edu

CONTENTS

FOREWORD

TASHA BERTRAM

I am delighted to be writing the foreword for this amalgamation of two very special books about Nicolas Legat. I was tremendously gratified to have set this republication in motion and now to have it come to fruition fills me with great joy. Although my generation was not taught by the great master himself, it is certainly true to say that once touched by Legat's essence, one is forever inspired to excel. It happened to me at the age of four, when I was taken to see a performance by John Gregory's Harlequin Ballet (a company of dancers trained in the Legat system). The experience was unforgettable, and it left me with a deep certainty that I, too, was going to dance. When I was ten, my dream was fulfilled and I became a full-time student at the Legat School in Mark Cross, East Sussex. The training was under the superb guidance of Moira Scott and the school's ballet principal, Eunice Bartell. Both were tremendous teachers who carried on the traditions of Nicolas's legacy through their work with his wife Nadine Nicolaeva-Legat.

Having been a student of the Legat system, a professional dancer, and now a teacher of his inspirational method, I know how essential it is for the next generation to be aware of his teachings. With this exquisite volume, we are invited to relish this work and enjoy the rich history of the creative genius who was Nicolas Legat.

You'll find in his *Memoirs* that he shares much of his knowledge and fills the pages with beautiful character descriptions as detailed as his art work and equally joyous. The subjects of his unique scrutiny include Gustav, his father; the legendary teacher Christian Johannsen; and the great choreographer Marius Petipa. We are also presented with a wonderful collection of photographs and a handful of his highly amusing and unique caricatures.

My introduction to these caricatures was at school, where prints from the original collection of nearly 100 by Nicolas Legat and his brother, Sergei, were hung all the way up the vast staircase. They were quirky and amusing to us as young ballet students and we all grew to love them. We would study them regularly and marvel at their joyful eccentricities. They became a continual reminder of Nicolas Legat's presence in our world, like the bronze bust of him in the school. We were sure that this beautiful sculpture captured his character exactly, as it sat in the main entrance hall displaying perfect épaulement. The bust now resides at the Royal Ballet School, displayed between busts of Dame Margot Fonteyn and Dame Ninette de Valois. A replica of this wonderful sculpture is at the Vaganova Ballet Academy Museum in St. Petersburg.

One of Legat's greatest talents was his capacity for recognizing individual potential. His ability to bring out the best in any dancer was a monumental part of the legacy that made him the unparalleled and inspiring teacher that he was. His wit and humor as an artist and his ethos as a master teacher filtered through all who knew him. As you'll see in *Heritage of a Ballet Master*, many great dancers express their gratitude and admiration for him.

Nicolas Legat set an invaluable standard for ballet education. I will always be indebted to the Legat system and I carry a part of him in everything I do. I am honored to have this opportunity to relaunch a record of his wisdom and beauty for the world to enjoy once more.

EDITOR'S PREFACE

MINDY ALOFF

Among the many out-of-print dance books in English that don't deserve obscurity, the second, 1939 edition of the memoirs of Nicolas Legat is a special treasure. Published in London, after the author's death and on the threshold of world war, this thin volume, well under 100 pages, contains elegant prose, remarkable information concerning the last three decades of St. Petersburg's storied Imperial Ballet, outstanding monotone photographic illustrations, some with loose tissue papers to protect them, and, most wonderfully, full-color prints of a handful of the celebrated caricatures of Imperial Ballet–era dancers and administrators that the author and his younger brother, Sergei, made. The color plates are handsomely printed in rich, matte colors. The paper for the text is thick and deckled; the binding is scarlet leather. As a grace note, the text of the memoirs is preceded by a poem about the ballet by John Masefield (1878–1967, poet laureate of Britain 1930–1967), anchored by a facsimile of the poet's signature.

A university press in the United States of the twenty-first century is not in a position to republish such a luxe volume using identical materials. However, the University Press of Florida is thrilled to be able to republish the book at all, after its many decades out of print. And four-color miniatures of some of Legat's watercolor caricatures can be seen online, at least giving a sense of how they look. Also, one can visit the full portfolio of ninety-five images owned by the Library of Congress and leaf through the actual Legat prints. In addition, The Jerome Robbins Dance Division of the New York Public Library for the Performing Arts owns an incomplete portfolio of eighty-six images.

It is also a pleasure to offer Legat's memoir in the company of another excellent book brought back into print: *Heritage of a Ballet Master: Nicolas Legat*, by two of Legat's erstwhile students who themselves became pedagogues: Ballet Russe dancer-choreographer John Gregory and the star danseur and founder of the Eglevsky Ballet, André Eglevsky. The heart of this volume are written records of complete classes devised by Legat and lovingly retained by Eglevsky. These classes keep company with delightful testaments by luminaries of twentieth-century ballet to Legat's genius as a teacher and an artist in several media.

Heritage was originally published by the specialty press Dance Horizons, which was overseen on East 26th Street in Brooklyn by its founder A. J. (Adolph, known as "Al") Pischl (1920–2019, also the co-founder, with Selma Jeanne Cohen, of the monograph series Dance Perspectives). During its twenty years as an independent publisher (1965–1985), Dance Horizons published around 150 titles. In 1986, it was purchased by the Princeton Book Company, which has kept in print or as e-books about 10 percent of the older publisher's extraordinary backlist on dance history, dance technique, and dance appreciation, issued in stylish, affordable paperback editions. Again, though, no comparably sized publisher today could afford to keep in print, in its entirety, that magnificently diverse list in terms of historical eras, dance traditions, and genres of approach—a list that included many republications of much older volumes, their subjects going way back past seventeenth- and eighteenth-century New England to the dances of the ancient world. It is a joy indeed to help bring back even one of Mr. Pischl's essential volumes.

Among the many individuals who worked to realize this double helping of Nicolas Legat's brilliance and sensibility, I want to single out the Legat devotee, dancer, and examiner Tasha Bertram, who brought us the idea of republishing the memoir; the English dance historian, collector, and author of *Tamara Karsavina: Diaghilev's Ballerina*, Andrew R. Foster, who has been of invaluable assistance to the marvelous scholar Robert Greskovic (who wrote the introduction) and to me; and the staff of the Jerome Robbins Dance Division at the New York Public Library for the Performing Arts, most especially Director Linda Murray and the Special Collections librarians.

INTRODUCTION

Nikolai Gustavovich Legat

ROBERT GRESKOVIC

Russian-born dancer, choreographer, visual artist, and ballet educator Nikolai Gustavovich Legat was 67 years old and living in England when, in a slightly different form, the memoir republished here was first released in a translation from the Russian by Sir Paul Dukes. The current reprint comes as the calendar marks the start of the third century of the legacy of Marius Petipa (1818–1910), who was ballet master of Russia's imperial ballet troupe from 1862 until 1903 and served as its ballet-master-in-chief from 1869. In his foreword to Legat's recollections, Dukes refers to the fact that in his prime, the memoirist was appointed as the immediate successor to the French-born Petipa, who continues to dominate the history of what is known as "classical" Russian ballet. Dukes's introductory text refers to Petipa as a "'deity of the choreographic art," likely taking the godhead designation from Legat's own mouth.

More later of the gods whom Legat revered and who loomed large in his life within the world of ballet until his death in London in 1937. But first a word about the English-born Dukes, who died in 1967 in Capetown, South Africa. His long-nosed and long-necked profile can be seen depicted near the beginning of the book in a black-pencil caricature by Legat. The August 28th *New York Times* obituary of Dukes makes no reference to the fact that he worked with Legat or to ballet at all, although he worked as a ballet trainee, albeit a late-starting one in his late 30s, under Legat's tutelage. In addition, the Englishman became one of the "other" men in Legat's marriage to dancer Nadine Nikolaeva (1895–1971). Instead, the obituary notice reflects on Dukes's career in the British Intelligence Service and the fact that on assignment in Soviet Russia he was known as "the man of 1,000 faces" because of his various disguises. In fact, the man who Englished Legat's writings, which were composed in the years immediately before 1932, was everything the *Times* text says. A man of some renown, Dukes was knighted in 1920 for his secret service exploits.

Educated in Russia, he spent years disguised as a workman, a soldier in the Red Army, and a member of the Communist Party before escaping to Lapland with the assistance of White Guards. In January 1914, no doubt wearing one of his Russian faces, Dukes found himself in the Mariinsky Theater in the presence of the emperor and his family. The occasion was Legat's 25th-jubilee performance, which presented Petipa's *Esmeralda*, with Legat as the poet Pierre Gringoire in the four-act ballet based on Hugo's *Notre Dame de Paris*. Legat's recollections note that the performance marked both his last time on the Mariinsky stage and the emperor's last visit to the theater.

Legat's memoir doesn't dwell too long on the dramatic political events and intrigues implied in Dukes's past, even though they directly led to the curtailment of Legat's career on stage and behind the scenes of the once-imperial ballet of Russia. Rather, what is here, in Dukes's English, is a loving recounting of Legat's training in the incomparable ballet world of tsarist St. Petersburg and of his performing there before he eventually emigrated and settled in England, largely at the urging of his wife, in 1922.

These are not reminiscences that detail the devastations of the violent revolution and upheaval that occurred in the wake of the October Revolution. And while some loss of artistic standards much concerns Legat as he looks back from his adopted home in England to the rigorous St. Petersburg ballet schooling and performing that had bred him, he largely and lyrically stresses the glories of Russia's way with ballet's art. Only in passing, on page 44 of his 56-page text, does he state that he "lost everything I possessed in the Revolution," and this in specific reference to having to leave Soviet Russia without even one copy of the now-famous album of vivid caricatures, first released in 1903 as *The Russian Ballet in Caricature*, "by the brothers Nicolas and Serge Legat." These insightful, witty, and sometimes unflatteringly accurate and astute depictions of individual physiques, visages, and expressions were drawn by Nicholas and his younger brother, Sergei, to document the on- and off-stage personnel of the Imperial Ballet.

Legat repeats his statement about losing his personal possessions when he notes that the violin used to accompany the demanding ballet lessons of his much-esteemed ballet teacher, Christian Johanssen (1817–1903, also spelled as Johansson)—which Johannsen's dancer-daughter Anna bequeathed to Legat—had been lost "with all my possessions in the Revolution." What he chose to leave out of his memoir is that—as stated in *The Legat Saga—Golden Years of the Russian Ballet: The Life and Times of Nikolai Legat* by John Gregory (first published in 1992, with a second edition in 1993)—the teacher's cherished instrument was smashed, with a diabolical laugh, over the knee of a Soviet Cossack thug who had taken up residence in Legat's home while he and Nikolaeva were away in Moscow. By this point in his story, we've been given select insights into Johannsen and his teaching methods as they impressed Legat while he was a member of the Imperial Ballet. Some of the caricatures selected for publication with this memoir come from the 1903 album of the Legat brothers' loose leaves, which the text calls "ninety-four cartoons." One is of Johanssen, brandishing his famous violin and bow and looking sleek and soigné in white tie, black satin tails, black patent-leather pumps, and black silk hose. Caricatures that Nicholas created of four individuals, including the legendary Sergei Diaghilev (1872–1929), whom Legat knew from his career outside Russia, postdate the lavishly published 1903 caricatures. Earlier in the memoir, Legat evocatively depicts Johannsen's teaching: "His class room became a real fairyland of movement, with the severe but benevolent old sorcerer waving his magic violin wand and awakening to life our most secret and often unlooked-for artistic capacities."

If, for Legat, Johannsen was the ultimate dancing master (that is, ballet pedagogue), Petipa was the supreme ballet master (that is, ballet choreographer). With no compunctions about or fear of sounding self-serving, Legat relates how his own choreographic and performing skills impressed Petipa. Eventually, Petipa trusted Legat to choreograph parts of his ballets. In particular, Legat notes, Petipa suggested that Legat both dance with Petipa's daughter Lubov (1880–1917) for her stage debut and set the dance they would be performing. And when the debut was over, with Legat's choreography, the proud aging ballet master told Legat, in halting Russian: "Da, ya vish ti mozh karasha composi," rendered in Dukes's English as, "Yes, I see thou able [to produce a] good compos[ition]."

During the time when the memoir was being translated into English and was initially published in England, what remained of the Russian ballet of Johanssen and Petipa, which Legat speaks of familiarly in matter-of-fact language, mostly remained behind the Iron Curtain, scarcely familiar to English-speaking readers. Much of what Legat recounts of the historic happenings in turn-of-the-twentieth-century Russian ballet has since been more thoroughly covered in historical and critical studies. Yet, this early firsthand depiction, complete with a palpable sense of its narrator's having been there, up close and personally in daily working relationship with Petipa, arguably the giant of ballet making in his time, resonates with a charm and color all its own.

Subsequent ballet histories of Legat's era in Russia—including the first two decades of the twentieth century, when the Imperial Ballet was evolving beyond its nineteenth-century traditions—are still emerging, as are more firsthand accounts of the ballet in that era by his contemporaries. Some of these texts, which are still only in Russian, await their friendly Paul Dukes treatment. For instance, in reading Legat's passing references to Michel Fokine (1880–1942), an innovator credited with making academic ballet more expressive and "new" in its time, I wonder if Legat's Russian is as mellow as Dukes's English. Fokine was once a student in Legat's own classes. Legat describes him as "one of his best pupils," and, as Fokine was eventually a choreographic force of note in the early twentieth century, he figures in his former teacher's recollections as an ultimately crucial figure, although perhaps with only grudging acceptance. In Dukes's translation, Legat avers that "as a producer" he himself "was never either iconoclast or pioneer of new forms" but rather was "simply a seeker of beauty in individuals."

Legat's teaching position at the Imperial Ballet School led to his soon succeeding Johannsen as professor of "the class of perfection," which is the standard English version of the "classe de perfectionnement," a designation established by the legendary school at the Paris Opera. The concept of such a class goes back to 1860–1870 in the tutelage of Marie Taglioni, the great Italian ballerina, who won lasting fame in Western Europe. As a dancer, teacher, and ballet master simultaneously connected to the Imperial Ballet's St. Petersburg home, the Mariinsky Theater, Legat shouldered a triple responsibility, which made his pay for his services the highest ever for an individual in the history of the Russian ballet. He points to this triple responsibility for St. Petersburg as the thing that kept him from accepting an invitation to join Diaghilev's Ballets Russes in 1910. This leads him to reflect as follows: "Perhaps, had I been able to see twelve years ahead, and had caught a vision of myself fleeing from the Bolsheviks with little but the clothes on my back, I might have chosen differently."

A good sense of Legat the teacher is much evidenced in André Eglevsky and John Gregory's *Heritage of a Ballet Master: Nicholas Legat*. Both Dukes's translation of the memoir and Eglevsky and Gregory's republication reproduce a caricature of the Legat brothers, made early on, studying at the barre in St. Petersburg under the watchful, stern eye of their teacher-father, Gustav Legat, shown accompanying their exercises on a violin as he drills them in dance moves. Large drops of sweat pour from the young men's foreheads. The *Heritage* publication opens with a foreword by beloved ballerina Alexandra Danilova (1903–1997) and includes tributes from some of the more prominent and grateful dancers who studied with Legat in the West, including Frederick Ashton, Anton Dolin, Alicia Markova, Léonide Massine, and Michael Somes.

But let's return to Fokine, who is now well-situated in ballet history as an innovator and creator of some historic ballets. Legat himself danced in two—*Petrouchka* and *Le Carnaval*—when he performed with Diaghilev's Ballets Russes in a brief stint during 1925. We now know from Russian sources that have recently been published, especially from the recently released diaries of Vladimir Telyakovsky (1861–1924), director of the Imperial Theaters at the beginning of the twentieth century, that Legat was decidedly antagonistic to Fokine during the century's first decade. A diary entry from April 16, 1909, notes that Legat's signature was included in a protest claiming "that ballet is going downhill due to the fact that parallel classes are introduced and taught by Fokine, who seems to violate the traditions of ballet and introduce new things."[1] As a dedicated Johannsen and Petipa champion and a member of the more conservative faction of St. Petersburg's ballet when Fokine was making waves on behalf of "new" forms, Legat wrote in his 1930s memoir that the "new" school of Fokine and others was, in fact, built on Petipa's established foundations.

The great Anna Pavlova, with whom Legat danced, is another ballet world figure with whom Legat had something of a falling out. Although his memoir and his career history show a decided reverence

1 Andrew Foster found and translated the Telyakovsky commentary for me.

for the ballerina, as his book amply demonstrates, some years before the book's publication Legat had been involved in an incident that qualifies as decidedly anti-Pavlova. In 1907, most likely in strong rebuke to criticism Legat had suffered at the hands of critic Valerian Svetlov (1860–1934), Legat penned and exhibited one of his more stinging caricatures. The watercolor shows Svetlov as a portly, white cockatoo, pushing an almost skeletal Pavlova in a three-wheeled phaeton. The image was meant to illustrate a trip the writer and his much-admired ballerina took to visit the tomb of Romeo and Juliet in Verona. In the watercolor, the Russians are shown carrying business cards to leave at the tomb.

In the early 1930s, Legat—seemingly in a more mellow mood—chose newer caricatures for inclusion in his memoir: one of Diaghilev as large-headed, doll-like figure; one of Kyra Nijinsky (1913–1998), daughter of the great and by-then-legendary Vaslav Nijinsky (1889–1950), whom, as the memoir relates, Legat immediately identified as a major talent when Nijinsky auditioned for the Imperial Theater School's dance division. Legat's muscled Kyra Nijinsky is dressed in 1930s practice garb and appears to be striding on air across the page. His depiction of the English-born Anton Dolin, at that time a budding ballet dancer, shows a bronzed, youthful athlete in an acrobatic handstand, wearing bathing briefs and ballet slippers with socks.

One of the memoir's more tantalizing surprises is a passage in which Legat confidently identifies a dancer who is otherwise unknown in the West as possessing prodigious gifts for classical dancing that made those of Nijinsky seem like "child's play." Dukes translated this dancer's name as "Domashoff." Although, along with describing several of the dancer's feats in the studio, Legat says only that he was a Moscow dancer, it is evident from other historical sources that the person he meant was Nikolai Petrovich Domashev (1861–1916 or 1917), who was a first dancer of Moscow's Bolshoi Theater from 1885 to 1906 and of whom Western ballet history needs to hear much more. Legat's point in discussing Domashev is not to call the evaluation of Nijinsky's abilities into question but rather to make the point that, as Dukes put it in English, there was "much talent that remained in Russia and never became known beyond her borders."

While the book's text includes an erratum note of its own, further corrections to the text are warranted. Most amusing is a slip-up that comes from Dukes's misunderstanding of what Legat says about the first cast of Petipa's iconic ballet, *The Sleeping Beauty*. We read that "Petipa himself played the role of the fairy Sirene." Now, "Sirene" refers to the key *Beauty* role of the Lilac Fairy, and the first interpreter of the part was Petipa's daughter Marie. However, Dukes has undoubtedly confused Legat's Russian for "M. Petipa" here to mean Marius Petipa rather than the Marie Petipa the author meant. Marius Petipa himself performed no role in his ballet.

There are also lesser misunderstandings or misreadings. The surname of the dancer identified as "Delera" should be spelled as Dell'Era, that is Antoinetta Dell'Era (1865–?), the first Sugar Plum Fairy in the Petipa-supervised *Nutcracker.* Translating Pavel Gerdt

(1844–1917), a longtime and revered danseur noble at the Mariinsky, as Paul Gerdt is not wrong, but it's also not standard usage nowadays: "Pavel" tends to be retained. With regard to his own performing of Petipa's *Sleeping Beauty*, Legat states that he "took part in practically every performance, playing at first the role of one of the bridegrooms [a.k.a., suitors to the Princess Aurora], and later that of the Prince Charming." Legat surely means Prince Désiré, since Prince Charming is the name of the character who accompanies the fairytale figure of Donkey-skin in the ballet's last act. (Although Diaghilev made a name change for Petipa's Prince Désiré in the Ballets Russes's 1921 production of *The Sleeping Princess*, Legat had no part in that production.) Legat's first mention of Petipa's famous assistant choreographer, Lev Ivanov, comes into the text here as "Leo." A pair of illustrations of Nijinsky is misidentified: The illustration on the right shows the dancer costumed as the title character in his ballet *Tyl Eulenspiegel* and not, as the identification reads, in Léonide Massine's *Le Tricorne*.

Some of the titles of the ballets named in the different lists of choreographic works Legat was connected with need adjusting. In Appendix 2, *Rozanna* should be *Roxanna*, *The King's Order* is usually called *The King's Command*, and *Deva Dunaya* refers to the Russian for *La fille du danube*. Elsewhere, *L'Adventure de Damis* should be *The Trial of Damis* or *Les Ruses d'amour*, *Galubaya Georgina* refers to *The Blue Dahlia*, *Waterman's Holiday* should more accurately be *Boatman's Holiday*, *Le Marche de Paris* should either be *Le Marché parisiene* or *The Parisian Market*, *Catherine* should read *Catarina*, *Love's Prank* is more accurately known as *Cupid's Prank*, *Nymph and Satyr* should be *Nymphs and Satyr*, and *The Purple Flower* is better named as *The Scarlet Flower* or *The Blood Red Flower*.

I acquired my copy of the 1939 memoir in 1979. At that time, Legat was largely a name on the pages of dance history and was arguably best known as a teacher. (His school, which Nikolaeva-Legat continued and is nowadays called The Legat School of Ballet and Contemporary Dance, is still in existence.) Legat's Russian ballet caricatures also gave substance to his name. However, the Legat name remained peripheral in the annals of twentieth-century choreography. His best-known choreographic effort, a 1903 remake with his brother, Sergei, of the broadly popular Viennese ballet from 1888, *Die Püppenfee*, known in Russia as *Feia Kukol* (*Fairy Doll*), helped place the Legat name in the history of ballet choreography. By my time, this once-famous and initially much-lauded work, which Legat dwelled on in one long paragraph of the memoir, mostly remained reduced to a somewhat cloying trio for an eyelash-batting ballerina in a bubble-gum pink tutu, supported by two whey-faced Pierrots, originally meant to be danced by Nicolas and Sergei themselves. Other than that, we can see his choreography in historic silent film footage of *La Nuit* (https://www.youtube.com/watch?v=ZunuLRTPfc0), as performed and reworked by Anna Pavlova from a duet Legat originally set for himself and the ballerina, and *Valse Caprice* (https://www.youtube.com/watch?v=dsm6qkTFtek) in a film that most likely recorded Legat's duet as danced by Alexandra Baldina (1885–1977) and Theodore Koslov (1883–1956), a dancer whom Legat says was especially grateful for his tutelage. The *Valse* isn't much to go on, although even its brief length manages to indicate the strict rigors, academically and plastically, that Legat held in high regard. To date there are no such records of Legat's stage performing, but the undated illustration at the start of his memoir showing him supporting Nikolaeva-Legat in *Lac de Cygnes* suggests that the danseur stayed too long on the boards, especially when compared with an earlier illustration of him opposite Pavlova in the same work.

From my perspective as a balletgoer and follower of ballet history, I find that it is Legat the teacher who claims the laurels for his name. Dukes's introduction stresses his subject's teaching and performing and gives no attention to his artwork or his choreography. Legat literature that postdates the memoir, prominently *The Legat Saga*, documents Legat's lack of enthusiasm for George Balanchine (1904–1983), a Russian-born ballet master who grew to international fame after a notable start with Diaghilev's Ballets Russes. A stanza in a poem Legat wrote that is included in *The Legat Saga* begins: "Now I see Balanchine / He had a bent back / He danced like a cook!"

My own admiration for Balanchine and his work puts him at the head of his class in the history of twentieth-century ballet. However, I found in the transcript of one of Balanchine's now-famous seminars for regional teachers at his School of American Ballet in 1960 and 1961 that the ballet master whom Legat saw in an unflattering light stated of Legat, "I myself studied with him" and noted that "he . . . taught very well." I accept, with extra confidence, the high regard for Legat voiced by those who knew his stage and classroom firsthand—such as Danilova, whose introduction to *Heritage of a Ballet Master* states: "He saw at once what we needed and he pushed us forward always forward." What I hear in this comment, starting with the use of "we" and not just "I," is that Danilova—who is known for her technical strength as well as for what she liked to call the "perfume" of performing—serves as an emblem of Nicolas Legat, who left his mark on any and all who sought his tutelage.

BALLET RUSSE

MEMOIRS OF NICOLAS LEGAT

Nadejda (Nadine) Nicolaeva and Nicolas Legat in "Lac de Cygnes"

BALLET RUSSE

MEMOIRS OF NICOLAS LEGAT

Translated, with a Foreword by Sir Paul Dukes, K.B.E.

Sir Paul Dukes, K.B.E. Translator of the memoir. Caricature by Nicolas Legat

FOREWORD

SIR PAUL DUKES

The translation of this book has given me immense pleasure, not only because it is the work of an old friend, but because, to use the current phrase, it fills a long-felt want. Several works exist on the Russian ballet as presented by Serge Diaghileff and on the Imperial Ballet from which Diaghileff's forces were first largely recruited, while a number of works have been devoted to individual dancers, but never before have we been told the inside story of how the school of dancing that lay behind the ballet came into being.

We have had the story of the stage, but we have never had the story of the class room. It is that story, the story of the class room, of the 'school,' that is presented to us in the following pages.

The author is the only living person capable of the task. The 'Legat Saga' is intimately related to the Imperial Theatres of St. Petersburg and Moscow for a hundred years past. Legat's father was professor before him, while he himself inherited the chair of the greatest dancing master of all time, Christian Johannsen, at the latter's personal insistence. For these reasons the story receives an added interest through the strong personal touch.

But not alone of the class room does Legat speak. He shows the intimate link between class room and stage. He was the successor not only to the 'deity' of the class room, Christian Johannsen, but also to the then 'deity' of choreographic art, Marius Petipa, and knowing both of them intimately, he reveals aspects of their characters and their workmanship which throw much new light on the part these titans played in the growth and development of the ballet.

Indubitably it is to be regretted that Legat did not see his way to give his talents to western Europe when Diaghileff first invited him to his nascent enterprise over twenty years ago. But was he to be blamed? He was the first ever to achieve the distinction of holding simultaneously the triple position of first soloist, ballet master, and professor of the highest class of the Ballet School. Moreover, Legat, though of Swedish descent, is essentially Russian to the core. He possesses none of that cosmopolitanism that prompted many other artists to leave Russia young, and exploit abroad the knowledge their schooling had given them. Clinging to Russian habits, customs, and manner of thinking, and having blazoned his name but little beyond the confines of his homeland, he is, unlike many others, less known to western Europe than to his native land, where the name of Legat was a household word in artistic circles throughout the length and breadth of the land.

I shall never forget a brilliant ballet evening at the Imperial Marinsky Theatre in the month of January 1914. It was one of the occasions for which it was quite impossible for any but the most influential to procure tickets, but M. Tartakoff, the director of the theatre and a good friend, relaxed so far as to allow me to stand just inside the door of the centre aisle. The audience was composed of the élite of the Russian nobility. The place blazed with jewels and uniforms. The strains of the National Anthem sounded, everyone rose, and all eyes were fixed on the Imperial box as the Tsar, the Tsarina, and the Imperial family entered and took their places. The orchestra, under Richard Drigo, broke into the overture and the curtain rose on the ballet *Esmeralda.* It was a gala night, but it was also more than that, it was a jubilee night. One by one the chief artists emerged to meet with warm receptions—the beautiful Matilda Kshesinskaya as Esmeralda, the dignified Paul Gerdt as Frolo, the celebrated mime Stukolkin as Quasimodo. Then about half-way through the first act, a slight figure in green jerkin, the poet Gringoire, was dragged on the stage by brigands. Suddenly the performance came to a stop. The entire auditorium rose to its feet. Even the Tsar stood. On the stage the performers deserted their positions to acclaim their colleague, who remained in the centre bowing incessantly, clearly moved to tears by this acclamation.

The poet Gringoire was Nicolas Legat, and the occasion the celebration of his jubilee of twenty-five years' service in the Imperial Theatre. The demonstration, which lasted a good fifteen minutes, and was repeated again in the next two acts, was a tribute of public admiration. In the last act, tables were brought on and piled with gifts and presents, while the hero of the day received address after address from countless organizations. One telegram read:

> 'Terpsichora tiem bogata
> Shto ti nam dala Legata.'
>
> ('*Terpsichore has shown her riches*
> *By giving us Legat.*')

And now, seventeen years later, that slight figure of the erstwhile poet Gringoire sits daily in his London studio, with infinite patience and kindly encouragement transmitting to others the art that raised him to such heights. It is above all in the studio that this artistic colossus is most at home. Since soloist days he is the teacher, the pedagogue *par excellence.* Modest and unassuming, invariably cheerful, carrying his sixty years as if they were thirty, keenly conscious of his profound knowledge not only of the externals of his art but also of the muscles of the human frame that execute the slightest movements—that knowledge which has made of him the foremost teacher of the Russian school of dancing since the death of Christian Johannsen—Legat with delicate hands adjusts an erring movement, directs

Nadine Nicolaeva-Legat

the exercises, or accompanies them with an endless variety of original tunes on the piano or violin. Out of hours he is fonder of 'swapping stories' or drawing comic cartoons than of 'talking shop.' He is one of those rare natures that never grow old. He is happiest of all with children, and amuses them just as years ago he used to amuse his colleagues with sleight-of-hand and juggling tricks on their long tours throughout Russia.

Like a noble and magnificent tree the Russian school of ballet has spread its branches throughout the world, and, as is usual with trees, it is for its foliage that it is chiefly admired. But the arborist looks deeper, he looks at the trunk and the roots. The roots of the Russian school were planted by his predecessors, but in Nicholas Legat we have the trunk.

Since writing the above introduction, Nicolas Legat has passed away, and with that passing the world lost its foremost exponent of the art of the Russian ballet.

In the final paragraph of this book Legat wrote these noble words:

> In the four quarters of the globe I behold the greatest dancers of my generation, many of them my pupils, upholding the standard of the Great Art, and if I am proud at the sight it is not merely a personal pride but a national pride, that we (Russians), in things material and political the despised and rejected of men, shall live for ever in thus transmitting a spark of the otherwise inexpressible soul of Russia. With this ideal I live, and with this ideal untarnished I shall die.

Legat kept his trust. To the last he lived with one ideal, one hope, one aim—to transmit his learning to succeeding generations and keep alight the torch so brightly lit in St. Petersburg in the last decades of the nineteenth century and the first decades of the twentieth.

But though the maestro is no more, his message has not died with him. The world is fortunate in that there was one fit to receive the torch from his hand. His wife, Madame Nicolaeva-Legat, referred to in these pages by her stage name of Nadine Nicolaeva, had the enormous advantage of exclusive training by Legat from her earliest youth. Nearly thirty years his junior, she received the full benefit of his most mature professorial years, acquiring the finest nuances and most delicate subtleties of his technique. Not content with this, she also addressed herself, when Legat retired from active work on the stage, to a study of modern character and even acrobatic dancing, perfecting herself in those forms of 'stylized' ballet dancing which came into vogue through the influence of Serge Diaghileff in his later years.

But Madame Legat never fell into the pitfall, as so many others have done, of allowing a craze for the grotesque, euphemistically described as the 'modern,' to blind her to the true values of her art. Long before the death of her husband she had begun to take his place as professor in his studio. More and more he entrusted to her hands his responsible work. Just as the venerable maestro Johannsen, in transferring his mantle to Legat, had sat at the latter's side to supervise his class, so Legat sat at the side of Nicolaeva; and as the austere and critical Johannsen pronounced Legat's work perfect, so Legat in turn pronounced hers. Nadine Nicolaeva-Legat is the direct inheritor of the mantle of the venerable Professor Johannsen.

It is this school, the Russian school of Johannsen and Legat, which to this day produces the premier dancers of Moscow and Leningrad. The present head of the Russian Theatrical Ballet School, Madame A. Y. Vaganova, received her training at the hands of Legat, and several of the elder dancers who are now carrying on and developing the tradition in Russia also passed through his class when he was director of the Class of Perfection. It must not be forgotten that Legat disliked leaving Russia even for temporary tours abroad, so that it is in Russia primarily that the Legat tradition was established. But the last fifteen years of his life were spent mainly in London, and here it is, fortunately for this country, that the highest treasures and most subtle secrets of his art are still handed down.

Sandra Monteith. Youngest pupil of the Legat School (4 years old)

CHAPTER ONE

WHENCE CAME THE 'RUSSIAN SCHOOL'?

The second half of the nineteenth century in Russia was marked by a florescence of art, music, literature, and science unparalleled in the history of the world.

During the first half of the century we were still under the powerful domination of foreign influences. It was to French, Italian, and German artists and composers that the Court looked for aesthetic guidance. Russia was dormant. The great bear was still hibernating, aesthetically the great bear was born and grew up hibernating, and none suspected the hidden powers in its silent massive form.

To the outside world Russia was a land of mystery, whose representatives, the few who travelled, were characterized by a strange breadth of vision, refinement of culture, and a manner of life distinguished by freedom from the trammels that commonly bound European society. Was not the 'Russian prince' a necessary figure in almost every mystery novel? But since these wandering Russian nobles adapted themselves with ease and grace to every European mode, Europe did not bother its head about the land that produced them. Whatever the 'princes' were, Russia was considered barbaric.

But with the rise of modern art in Europe, Russia suddenly awoke, burst into life, leapt into astounding activity, and in every branch of intellectual life not only kept abreast of Europe, but often outran her.

The 'Russian school' of literature with Pushkin, Lermontoff, Gogol, Dostoevsky, Turgenev, Tolstoy, and Chekhoff became a European craze. The 'Russian school' of painting, from Vereschagin, Repine, Aivasovsky, Seroff to Roerich and Bakst, established new models in art. The 'Russian school' of music, with Tchaikovsky still betraying his homage to the Italian cult, soon shook itself free from this tutelage, and in Balakirev, Borodin, Moussorgsky, Rimsky-Korsakoff, and Glazounoff proved its complete independence and unique originality. And side by side with these was born the 'Russian school' of dancing, culminating in that superb and unprecedented phenomenon, the Imperial Russian Ballet.

Whence came this 'school'? Who made it? Whose genius formed and modelled it?

Ballet existed in Russia long ago. Rich land magnates kept their own dancing troupes and presented their best dancers to the Court. Thus originated the Court Ballet, which later became the Imperial Ballet. For technical guidance, in dancing as in other arts, authorities were invited from abroad. Among the best known ballet masters of the early part of last century were the Frenchmen Didelot and Perrot. The former became a rich man and established a scholarship for the Imperial Theatre School. I was one of the winners of this scholarship and thus paid my way through the Theatre School.

The secret of the development of Russian dancing lay in the fact that we learnt from everybody and adapted what we learnt to ourselves. We copied, borrowed from, and emulated every source that gave us inspiration, and then, working on our acquired knowledge and lending it the stamp of the Russian national genius, we moulded it into the eclectic art of the Russian ballet.

From the beginning of the second half of the last century the scene is dominated by two masterly figures—Marius Petipa, the choreographer, and Christian Johannsen, the professor. Both lived to a great age, and between them were mainly responsible for that perfection of development of individual technique and choreographic construction which arrived at full bloom in the first quarter of the present century. It is upon the foundation laid by these two men that the 'new' school of Fokine and others was built.

In a later chapter I shall deal in detail with these outstanding personalities, both of whom I knew intimately. Here I will merely pause to point out that neither of them was Russian by birth, though both became Russian by adopted nationality. Petipa was a Frenchman. His father before him occupied the post of first *maître de ballet* of the Russian Imperial Theatres, and Marius succeeded to the post. Christian Johannsen, who for over sixty years was professor of the Theatre School, was a Swede. He was a pupil of Bournonvilles (father and son), who in turn were pupils of Vestris. The French succession was also handed down to my father, Gustav Legat, who was professor of the Imperial Theatre School in Moscow. He was the most trusted pupil of Johannsen before myself, and when Johannsen could not accept private engagements he always put my father in his place. My mother was Russian, but my father, like Johannsen, was a Swede, though he and Johannsen always spoke French together. But my father's mother, my grandmother, was Constance Lede, a Frenchwoman, and a brilliant dancer in her time.

Christian Johannsen always used to say to me: 'The Russian school is the French school, only the French have forgotten it.' How true this was I discovered when I came to make my début at the Paris Grand Opera. I was dancing with Matilda Kshesinskaya and we were very nervous, for Russians were still regarded as semi-barbarians at the beginning of this century. Before the rehearsal we keenly felt the supercilious attitude of our French colleagues. But when they saw our work, what a sensation! What stupefaction was caused! Mme. Mory, then chief ballet mistress at the Grand Opera, fell on our necks and exclaimed: 'Voilà des vrais danseurs, jamais je n'ai vu pareils!' And the then assistant ballet master, Leo Staats, asked me: 'Tell me, please, what school is yours?' If any question could have astonished me, it was surely this! But I answered the simple truth. 'Yours,' I said, 'your school, the French school, which you have lost, but which we Russians have not only preserved but have poured into it our Russian soul!'

Staats asked to be allowed to work with me, and I consented with pleasure. But his study did not last long; in twenty minutes of my ordinary exercises he was exhausted, excused himself on the ground of not feeling well, and that was the end of his lessons!

Though the Russian school first derived its technique from France, it had already acquired by the middle of last century an international aspect through the influential personalities of Johannsen and my father, and through guest-performers from many parts of Europe. Taglioni, Grisi, Fanny Elssler, and others became in turn the idols of Russian balletomanes. Especially in the 'eighties a number of brilliant Italian dancers came to Russia, and as their names are still fresh in the memory of the present generation, and their influence gave a powerful impetus to the growing art of ballet at the time, I intend to deal first with this group of dancers and the part they played.

The first of this group was Virginia Zucchi, whom I remember very well, appearing with her in minor roles on the stage in my youth. She danced first at a suburban pleasure-garden or music-hall on the outskirts of St. Petersburg. She had a captivating personality and powerful talent, both for drama and comedy, which made so strong an appeal that she received an invitation to appear as a guest on the Imperial stage, and was later accepted into the ballet company. I remember her best in *Esmeralda* and *Pharaoh's Daughter,* in the latter of which I played, as a pupil, the part of the monkey. Zucchi always aroused my inexpressible admiration for her marvellous mimicry, her hypnotic acting. Her success led to other Italians being invited to various theatres in Russia (Italian opera and drama in St. Petersburg were at their height, and this gave the Italians added popularity). Zucchi was followed by Brianza, Delera, Limido, Cecchetti, Coppini (ballet master), Legnani, and Grimaldi. With the younger of these ballerinas, Legnani and Brianza, I danced as partner in my young days. With the others I took part on the stage in minor roles. But I see them all before my mind's eye as if it were yesterday.

The only male dancer of the Italian group was Enrico Cecchetti. He was about forty-five years of age when he came to Russia, and at the very height of his career, but too old to modify his school of *tours de force,* or round out his dexterity with the dignity and poise which were then the outstanding attributes of the Russian school. The first time I ever saw him dance was at a music-hall in the pleasure-garden Arcadia. I was sixteen at the time. To say that I was dazed by what appeared then to be the amazing virtuosity of the little Italian would be expressing it mildly. I came out literally staggered. Eight pirouettes! And on the stage of the Imperial Marinsky Theatre and in the Theatre School our dancers were content with four!

Cecchetti was partnering Limido, and these two made a perfect combination. They were both very small, but graceful and well built. Limido was, in my opinion, the greatest of all the Italians and one of the greatest dancers of all time. In pure technique she excelled all others, and it was wellnigh incredible that when she came to Russia she was already fifty years of age. Cecchetti was referred to in the Press as 'that bone-splitting specialist of vertiginous dexterity.' My father used to take me to see this remarkable pair every day. I had just entered the senior class of the Theatre School at the time, and at my request my father introduced me to Cecchetti, and I stood long shaking his hand, expressing in ardent terms my youthful admiration. When I had graduated and was a soloist in the Marinsky Theatre, Cecchetti and I became great friends.

All these dancers, when they came to Russia, were in their prime. We found that they had a school all their own, which was distinguished by remarkable dexterity and sensational brilliance. Their tours, their pirouettes, their *fouettés* were all superior to our own. Their manners, on the other hand, often lacked grace; theirs was a school of *tours de force;* taste was sacrificed to effect and dexterity. But we Russians had not invited them to criticize them. We readily acknowledged their technical superiority, and promptly set about to imitate, adapt, and ultimately to excel their technique.

From that moment onward we set ourselves the deliberate goal of learning the Italian tricks. In our spare time we turned pirouettes and double *tours* for hours, sometimes until we were even on the point of fainting. At the same time I lost no opportunity of watching the Italians, especially Cecchetti and Legnani, at their work, observing the holding of their body and which muscles they controlled. I learnt a great deal from these observations. Already, when I was given my début at the Marinsky Theatre, double *tours, entrechat-huits,* six or seven pirouettes were pretty easy for me, and the newspapers said that all the prior generation of dancers, including Cecchetti, would have to look to their laurels. But the climax of our technical achievements was not reached until considerably later.

The leaders in this movement to outdo the Italians in their own speciality were my brother Serge, Egor Kyasht, and myself, and we were eagerly followed by all the dancers of our generation. The advantage of this friendly rivalry was all on our side, for whereas the group of Italian dancers were all in their prime, finished dancers of thirty-five to fifty years of age, we of the succeeding Russian generation were young and burning with desire to learn—to learn from anywhere and anyone. We were fresher and physically stronger. I remember once when my brother and I were wrestling in our dressing-room, Cecchetti looking on (we shared the same dressing-room), said: 'I'll put either of you "puppies" down like a feather.' I let him try on me for a time, and then, making an effort, I lifted him with one arm and pinned him to the floor. (In my best days I lifted 150 pounds with one hand.) But this rivalry in no way affected our friendship or the respect and admiration of the 'puppies' for the full-bred 'lions.' Enrico Cecchetti was a great dancer, and we owe an inestimable debt to all the Italians who gave such an impetus to our art forty years ago.

Among the Italian dancers a special position was occupied by Legnani. She was one of the later arrivals, and the only one who manifested a desire to learn from the Russians. The others considered the technical equipment they had brought with them all-sufficing. Legnani, being nearer our own generation, continued to study.

At her début in the ballet *Zolushka* there was a dramatic pause in the coda. Legnani walked to the centre of the stage, signalled to the conductor, and executed thirty-two *fouettés* in one spot. The feat brought the house down, and marked an epoch in the progress of pure technique on our own stage.

To appreciate the overwhelming effect of this purely technical and nowadays common dancing trick on the balletomane audiences of that time, the reader must imagine the atmosphere of the period. It was the period of bloom of Russian art and Russian literature. New schools, new tendencies, new groupings of thought were springing up on every hand. Every striking new departure was hailed either as a step towards artistic or philosophic liberation by its supporters, or denounced by effervescent critics as a plunge into perdition. But nothing was received with indifference. In the realm of ballet the Italians had given a tremendous impulse to Russian art by their specific development of technique. Our dancers, male and female, our balletomane critics, even our professors raved technique, and when Legnani, first performed this hitherto unknown *tour de force,* she left both colleagues and spectators stunned.

Cecchetti was now teaching, and our dancers flocked to him to learn the Italian technique, and especially the thirty-two *fouettés.* But try as they might, they were unable to acquire this trick. Legnani, however, was a very great friend of mine, and I was her favourite partner. Prior to dancing with me Legnani danced by preference with Paul Gerdt, but one day, when Gerdt had sprained his ankle, Petipa appointed me in his place, and from that moment Legnani and I became almost inseparable stage companions. She was anxious to round off the Italian angularity of her dancing by acquiring Russian poise and line; I was anxious to acquire the Italian technique and adapt it to our school. We became working comrades and for three years practised together daily in the same studio. All this time I observed her closely.

Our star ballerina at the time was Matilda Kshesinskaya. She too struggled to acquire from Cecchetti the famous thirty-two *fouettés.* But neither he nor Legnani herself were able to make her do it. One day, when I was watching, I said to Matilda: 'Try it like this,' and I put her in a certain position. 'Tighten this muscle, and at every turn relax and contract it, making such and such a movement with the head.' Up to that time she always fell about the seventh or eighth turn. The first time she tried my method she turned about a dozen times. Then she began working with me systematically, and soon acquired the thirty-two *fouettés* to perfection. A short time later she did Legnani's feat on the Marinsky stage amid indescribable enthusiasm. And on the following morning I received a gift of a gold cigar-case and a note of grateful thanks from a certain very exalted personage.

Legnani was as mystified as Kshesinskaya that a youthful Russian was able to teach the most sensational of the Italian tricks. But the secret was simple. I had observed very closely, and had discovered exactly how Legnani held her body. After that many of our dancers came to me to learn Italian technique. I taught *the fouettés* to Vera Trefilova, Vil, Vaganova; later to Nicolaeva and many others, and now it is a common feat. And I found I also had

M. Kshesinskaya, by Nicolas Legat

success with the men. My brother graduated six years after me. All these years I trained him in special technique, while my father carried on his general instruction, and at his final examination from the Theatre School, Serge Legat executed fourteen *coup de pied* pirouettes at one stroke.

From now onward, though we continued to acknowledge the priority of the Italians both on account of age and precedence, we no longer doubted that we should acquire all they had to give and greatly improve their school. The embellishments they offered were accepted not only by us, the eager aspirants of the succeeding generation, but also by the teachers of the Theatre School, and incorporated into the Russian system. The trick of holding the head to the audience during pirouettes, for instance, was at once adopted by Johannsen, Petipa, my father, and all the Russian teachers. It was only when they saw the stage occupied by a group of Italians sacrificing everything to a display of fireworks that those old titans, Johannsen and Petipa, would hang their heads.

The desire to exploit Italian technique to the utmost was exemplified by the invitation to Enrico Cecchetti to form a class at the Imperial Theatre School. It was referred to as the 'parallel' class, and was for girls only. Cecchetti was as brilliant a teacher as he was dancer, exceedingly thorough and painstaking, though terribly hot-tempered. But he taught the Italian style only, and if the class lasted only a few years it was certainly not because the Italians were not good pedagogues, but because the Russians quickly assimilated the Italian technique and lent it that superior grace which was the heritage of the Russian school.

For many years Cecchetti became one of the most prominent figures in the ballet world in St. Petersburg. His pupil Albertieri acted for a time as his substitute, and I remember how the hot-tempered Cecchetti in a fit of anger would chase the unfortunate Albertieri brandishing a stick or violin-bow or anything that came to his hand, and five minutes later they would shed tears of reciprocal contrition.

They were great people, those Italians, and we loved them dearly. But there was one striking difference between them and the two greatest figures of the time, Petipa and Johannsen, who were building up what finally became the Russian school. Whereas both of the latter became Russian, Cecchetti and his compatriots never did so; they came to Russia Italians, lived there as Italians, and left Italians, scarcely able to speak the Russian language despite their years of residence, and absorbing nothing of the national character.

Nevertheless, lest I lay myself open to misunderstanding, let me repeat that I consider we owe as great a debt to the Italians as to the Scandinavians and the French, from whom our teachers, our ballet masters, and our original school sprang; and none is more willing than I, who spent years in copying them, to acknowledge it. But the mistake of the Italians was to rely almost exclusively upon technique and virtuosity in their dancing. Carried away by the sensation these caused, they regarded them as all-sufficing. They came to Russia too late to unlearn them, and without in any way depreciating the high qualities of the Italian dancers, it none the less remains a reflection upon the Russian school to say that it does not differ essentially in certain respects from the Italian.

E. Cecchetti, by Nicolas Legat

Without embarking in this limited space on an analysis of the two systems, it may be said briefly that the differences lie, firstly in principle, and secondly in taste. One of the principles of the Russian school is that of balanced training; the Italians, on the contrary, permitted a great deal of one-sidedness for the sake of superficial effect. Enrico Cecchetti, for example, though a brilliant pirouettist, could only do pirouettes and *tours en l' air* in one direction. We used sometimes to tease him into trying the other direction, and this would make him angry. A series of double *tours* in alternate directions, often done by our dancers, was beyond him. Our dancers eventually did seven or eight pirouettes habitually in their solos, but they did them in either direction at will. Whether they outdid others in this or not was merely incidental, it was the principle of balanced training that was at stake. We rejected a number of easy effects obtained at the cost of beauty and grace, and we avoided those faults *of épaulement* and carriage which are always marked in the Italian school. To the untrained eye these differences may appear insignificant. But it was our refusal to sacrifice aesthetics to effect, combined with our success in adopting and adapting Italian technique, that enabled us in the generation that followed the arrival of the Italians in Russia to produce the greatest dancers of the past four decades.

Thus the 'Russian' school of dancing is an eclectic school—the French, the Scandinavian, the Italian—all welded into an artistic whole by the genius of the Russian people in the age of art and letters that produced also Tchaikovsky and Rimsky-Korsakoff, Tolstoy and Turgenev, Repine and Bakst. . . . But there is this distinction between composers, writers, and painters on the one hand and dancers on the other, that the art of the latter cannot be recorded on canvas or on paper; it lives in our bodies and in our hearts; and paying homage to all from whom we derived our art, it is for us of that great generation to hold the torch aloft, and with it light coming generations on their way.

Anna Pavlova and Nicolas Legat in "Lac de Cygnes"

CHAPTER TWO

THE MEN WHO MADE THE RUSSIAN SCHOOL

I have spoken first of the Italian because, being the latest, they were also the best known of the foreign groups of artists who influenced the Russian ballet. But it must not be supposed that they in any way held a monopoly of our stage, despite the craze of the 'eighties and early 'nineties for Italian ballet, opera, music, and Italian art in general. There were great contemporary dancers of our own school, too, who in some respects were superior to the Italians.

Particularly I recall E. Vazem, E. Sokolova, M. Gorshenkova, all pupils of Johannsen. Among the men, Stukolkin was the great mime of that period, and among classic or character dancers there were many who were distinguished: Felix Kshesinsky, Gustav Legat, Platon Karsavin (father of Tamara Karsavina), Paul Gerdt (her godfather and teacher), Litavkin, Hillert, Bekefy. . . .

The younger of the above-named men, such as Gerdt and Bekefy, I always think of as of my own period, for though they were older than myself I was almost immediately classed with them at the commencement of my career on the Marinsky stage.

My family's association with the Imperial Ballet dates back over hundred years. My grandfather, who was a Swede, was invited into the Imperial Ballet company by the Emperor Nicolas I.

Long, long ago this connection began, in the reign of Nicolas I, when People's Theatres used to be constructed in St. Isaac's Square and on the Field of Mars at St. Petersburg. Popularly these theatres were called *balagani.* The first scene of Stravinsky's ballet *Petroushka* shows the outside of a *balagan,* and the shows were given in a tent or a portable wooden structure. They were run by my grandfather and his brothers, Ivan and Samuel Legat, known as the 'inseparables.' Ivan was the ballet master and scenic designer, and Samuel the engineer. Their first shows bore a somewhat military character, but they soon introduced pantomimes, with all kind of transformations, disappearances, and tricks. Then they introduced dancing, and here, under a pseudonym, my father made his first appearances. He danced with his mother, Constance Lede, who was slim and small and just the right height for him. He was Harlequin and she Columbine. These *balagani* became quite an institution, and were visited by the Tsar on several occasions. Artists of the Imperial Theatres also often came to see the performances.

At that time there was a renowned bass, by name Petroff, who sang at the opera. On the occasion of his jubilee performance it was decided to give Weber's opera, *Freischütz.* Petroff begged the director of the Imperial Theatres to invite Ivan and Samuel to produce the magician scene of this opera, and thus they were introduced to the Imperial Stage. Their creations caused a great sensation, and the Tsar Nicolas I, who was present, gave them each a gold watch with his initials, and at his command they became permanent members of the company.

Christian Johannsen, impelled by the mystery of Russia and the growing interest in Russian art, came to St. Petersburg from Sweden when still a youth about the end of the first quarter of the last century. He was a pupil of the famous Bournonvilles, who in their turn were pupils of the still more famous Vestris. While the Russians assimilated and perfected the distinctive features of the French and Italian schools, on the pedagogic side there is a clear heritage through the Bournonvilles, Johannsen, Gustav Legat, and myself from Vestris. This explains why we excelled, not only in developing the art of the ballet to the highest degree, but also in transmitting it to others. Once settled in Russia, Johannsen never again left the country. He became naturalized, took a Russian wife, and learnt the language well, with only a slight accent. His success as a dancer was secured from his first appearance and he was at once accepted into the Imperial troupe. He was of a most hardy constitution, and never wore more than a thin cotton jacket. He used to relate how, soon after he first came to Russia, one fine winter day he was walking down the Nevsky Prospect, keenly enjoying the frosty air, when a policeman stopped him, seized a handful of snow, and started rubbing his nose with it energetically. Johannsen's nose was frozen white, and the policeman had noticed it, though he himself had not!

He kept his robust health even into advanced old age, and I never heard of his having a day's illness. I remember, when he was about eighty, his entering the school building with Marius Petipa, then about seventy-five. With the agility of a man of forty Johannsen ran up the stairs two steps at a time, and turning round to laugh at Petipa laboriously mounting, chaffed him with: 'Eh starik!' ('Oh, you old 'un!'). Among a collection of literature I lost in the Revolution was a report of an appearance of Johannsen at the age of fifty-nine. This report said: 'This remarkable dancer has made still further progress.' Still further progress—at fifty-nine! Of such stuff were made the men who made the Russian school.

But I personally knew him, of course, only as a teacher. The figure I remember is one of medium height, sturdy, with a powerful chest, grey hair and thick eyebrows, light-blue eyes, a small hooked nose, and a short cut moustache and beard.

He was a brilliant dancer in his younger days, my father always told me, his dancing being characterized by great energy and life combined with perfection of finish. Even in his older days, when I worked under him in the class room, he would astonish us occasionally by demonstrating

C. Johannsen, by Nicolas Legat

without any practice a chain of steps, ending up with a series of flashing pirouettes, and come suddenly to a dead standstill in an irreproachable arabesque. There was something positively uncanny about it.

He was extremely methodical and unfailingly regular in his habits. He was always in the class room ahead of time, and prepared the floor himself by watering it. Then he would take his violin, seat himself at the end of the room, and curtly open the class after the minimum of preliminary civilities.

He hated smoking and used to say: 'Ugh, why do you tear your lungs to bits with that filth!' But he himself loved snuff, and took copious pinches of it.

He was very sparing in words, severe in his criticism, and laconic in his condemnations. The very highest compliment he ever paid anyone was: 'Now you may do that in public.' And the pupil then knew he had achieved perfection. So that many of our artists were afraid of Johannsen, and indeed his tuition was for none but those who with perseverance and enthusiasm aimed at the highest. Towards others he was ruthless and sarcastic. From the first I felt a passionate devotion to this grand old man and a keen insight into his methods. I became his favourite pupil, and worked many happpy hours with him out of school time. He used me as his assistant and delegated work to me long before he retired. From him I acquired the very essence of his school, and found myself imitating many of his manners, even to the preference for accompanying my instruction on the violin rather than the piano. If I drew the line anywhere, it was only in not imitating his overawing severity. I love to encourage my pupils, and not to reprimand them in their difficulties.

In his teaching Johannsen exhibited the most extraordinary versatility, ingenuity, and variety. In this he differed from the Italians who taught in Russia, and whose method of teaching was much more stereotyped. Enrico Cecchetti, for instance, even had hanging on his class room wall a sort of menu of exercises for the week: Monday such-and-such movements, Tuesday such-and-such, and so on. This system was severely criticized by Johannsen, who declared that it displayed paucity of imagination, stunted the inventive faculty, and led to too mechanical development. As for himself, it was said that in all the sixty odd years of his professorship in Russia, he never gave two lessons alike or repeated the same combination of exercises twice.

It was this inexhaustible ingenuity, combined with a penetrating insight into the peculiarities and possibilities of individual pupils, that made study under Johannsen a fascinating experience in itself. His class room became a real fairyland of movement, with the severe but benevolent old sorcerer waving his magic violin wand and awaking to life our most secret and often unlooked-for artistic capacities.

How many thousands upon thousands of combinations of steps he invented on the spur of the moment, weaving them into nets of bewitching line and motion—and never the same twice! Some of our pupils tried to write down these combinations and record them. But Johannsen did not encourage this. His combinations and chains of steps were inspirations of the moment, designed for the moment, and for individuals of the moment. By stereotyped repetition from record they must inevitably suffer. What he encouraged in his pupils was the faculty to invent and combine chains of steps for themselves.

What Christian Johannsen was as professor, Marius Petipa was as ballet master and producer. Between them these men dominated the development of the Russian ballet during the entire second half of the nineteenth century, and formed the Russian school as we knew it up to the time of the Great War. The one was the deity of the class room, the other of the stage, and their word in their respective departments was absolute.

Marius Petipa (or Petipas, as the name was originally in French) was never invited to Russia: he came of his own accord, prompted by his natural initiative, and his arrival was typical of the man. His father was *maître de ballet* of the Imperial Theatre before him, and he was told to invite his son Ivan, a good classic dancer, from Marseilles. Not to be outdone in 'the rush to Russia' of the period, the enterprising Marius turned up ahead of his brother and stole his job.

Marius Petipa did not excel as a classic dancer, but was an agile and talented interpreter of character dancing, distinguishing himself especially in Spanish dances, which he studied in Spain. He was also a splendid actor and an able supporter.

After the death of his father he succeeded to the post of ballet master of the Imperial Theatres. He settled in Russia permanently, became a Russian subject, lived there over seventy years, served under four Emperors, and was awarded many decorations.

Young, handsome, gay, and gifted, to the end of his days an inveterate *bon viveur,* he at once won popularity among the artists. He was the life and soul of every gathering, and kept things always on the go by his stories, jokes, and juggling abilities, which he was fond of demonstrating at table. My earliest recollections of him date from my childhood. He was godfather to one of my sisters, and a great friend of my family. I was very fond of him and very devoted to him.

But in his profession he was very severe, and never allowed the least favouritism. Though he finally gave me the principal roles in his later ballets, and I set many *pas de deux* for him that passed under his name, he never paid much attention to me in my youth. I had to prove my worth first, and I was over twenty-six before he gave me a leading role. But after I had set the début dances, first of his daughter Lubov, then of Tamara Karsavina, and one or two others, he called upon me more and more and I became thoroughly permeated with his ideas. One of his favourite compositions was a *pas de trois* in the ballet *Paquita,* which was danced by Kshesinskaya, Anna Johannsen, and myself. Petipa used to call this his 'golden *pas de trois.*' 'Imposs better tance!' he used to say in broken Russian.

Altogether Petipa produced some one hundred and fifty ballets, besides many *pas de deux* and solo numbers. His speciality was women's solos. Here he excelled by his mastery and taste. All his ballets were distinguished by variety of character and great imagination.

As a single instance of Petipa's work I will describe the creation of Tchaikovsky's famous ballet, *The Sleeping*

Marius Petipa

Beauty. This ballet was staged by direct order of the Emperor Alexander III. I shall never forget how Petipa tested the patient Tchaikovsky to the utmost with his capricious exactions. More accustomed to the orthodox forms of Pugni and Minkus, Petipa at first found it difficult to adapt himself to the famous Russian composer's novel arrangements, and constantly demanded that *tempos* should be altered and cuts and additions made, with all of which demands Tchaikovsky obligingly complied.

On the opening night the role of the Sleeping Beauty was performed by the Italian ballerina Brianza. The four bridegrooms were Karsavin, Oblakoff, Gillert, and myself. Gerdt was the Prince and Cecchetti the Witch. Petipa himself played the role of the Fairy Sirene. The Bluebird was Varvara Nikitina, and her partner Cecchetti. The Good Fairies were Anna Johannsen, Kulitchevskaya, Zhukova, and Rikhliahova. The Cats were played by Anderson and Bekefy. Many others later played the leading role, among them being Kshesinskaya, Preobrazhenskaya, Trefilova, Karsavina, and Anna Pavlova. The last named, however, was not fond of this role, there being too little mimicry in it for her liking. Her favourite ballet was *Giselle,* in which her acting talent found brilliant scope, and where in the second act, in the cemetery, she was able to display her ethereal inspired dancing.

Whenever Petipa set about producing a ballet he waited till absolute silence reigned in the hall. Then, consulting the notes he had composed at home, he would methodically begin work. He worked out many of his groupings at home, where he used little figures like chess pawns to represent dancers, arranging them all over the table. He would spend long hours studying these groupings and write down the successful ones in his notebook. Separate numbers, solos, and *pas de deux* he composed at the rehearsals.

First he had the music played through. He would sit for a time in deep thought. Then he would usually ask for the music to be played again, imaging the dance, making little gestures, and moving his eyebrows. In the middle he would jump up and cry: 'Enough.' He would then compose the dance eight bars at a time, call the dancer to him, and explain the movements at first in words rather than gestures. The whole dance having been explained, the dancer began again from the beginning, while Petipa frequently stopped, corrected, or modified the movements. In the end he would say: 'Now try nice,' which meant the artists might try to execute the finished dance.

For women Petipa was the ideal dance composer. He had an amazing capacity for finding the most advantageous movements for each danseuse, so that the end result looked both simple and graceful. He rarely gave combinations involving high technique, but paid chief attention to grace and beauty of line and pose.

For men, he was unable to compose effective dances. We almost always had to modify or develop them to suit our style, and we used to consult Johannsen on this, he being for men what Petipa was for women as a dance composer.

The most fascinating moments of all were those when Petipa composed his mimic scenes. Showing each participant in turn he would get quite carried away by the parts, and the whole hall would sit with

Vera Trefilova

bated breath, following the extraordinary expressive mimicry of this artistic giant. When the scene was set there would be a terrific outburst of applause, but Petipa paid little attention. He would return quietly to his seat, smiling and licking his lips in a characteristic gesture, lighting a cigarette, and sitting silent for a time. Then the whole scene would be repeated while Petipa put finishing touches to the actions of the individual artists.

The Sleeping Beauty was one of Petipa's most successful productions. More than two hundred performances were given in my time, always with enormous success. I took part in practically every performance, playing at first the role of one of the bridegrooms, and later that of the Prince Charming.

Although he lived more than seventy years in Russia, Petipa never learned to speak the language properly, though he understood all that was said to him. It was amusing to hear him give instructions. Bystanders often could barely refrain from laughing. For instance, when he was selecting artists for certain roles he would go up to them, stare long through his spectacles, and finally say: 'Ya dum ke ti moj probrop!' (Which might be rendered thus: 'I tink thou able try!'—TRANS.)

He said 'thou' to everybody because he had known us all at school. When anyone made a mistake at rehearsals he would shout out: 'Stoi, stoi, kakoi nistchas madam, kakoi ti skvern ogurtsi!' (Which might be rendered: 'Stop, stop, what miserable madam, what you are bad cucumber!') To a question from a woman soloist, who thought she had done wonderfully, Petipa snapped: 'Ni gratz, ni elevatz, kakoi nistchaz!' (A rhyme which might be rendered: 'No grace, no spring, what sorry thing!') His exclamations when he got angry were often quite unparliamentary.

Much was written about Petipa to explain his 'system,' but most of it was quite beside the point. This was his system, to look for beauty, grace, and simplicity, and obey no other rules. To change an artist or the number of participants was in his eyes to change the production, so that to imitate him with other material was to travesty him. Moreover, his greatness lay partly in that he recognized his limitations. A genius for women's solos, he rarely set men's dances well. He knew this, and did not object to our consulting Johannsen about them, while in Petipa's later ballets I set a good many of the men's solos and *pas de deux*.

I never made any deep philosophical analysis of his methods, perhaps because words and analyses don't interest me. It was enough for me that when Petipa had no time to set some new dance that had been ordered he would call me and say: 'Eto ti diel' ('You do it'). And I did it, proud that the dance should pass under his name. And 'Marius,' as we all spoke of him, always said afterwards, 'Da, ti karasha composi' ('Yes, you composed well').

To get ideas for the men's solos, Petipa would often sit through Johannsen's class, fingering his pencil and notebook. And after class Johannsen would wink and say: 'The old man's pinched some more.' (Johannsen would never admit that he himself was old!)

These two titans, Petipa and Johannsen, so dissimilar in character, were none the less good friends, and admired each other. There was a sardonic dryness about them. They lived for their work and ignored the conventionalities. When Johannsen's friend and colleague, Leo Ivanoff, instructor of the Junior Class, died at the age of about seventy, I came to tell Johannsen the sad news. Instead of saying, 'Oh, how sad,' he burst out laughing. 'Ha, ha, ha,' he exclaimed, shaking a forefinger, 'it must have been his debts strangled him!'

Petipa was similar. When Johannsen died at the age of ninety-four the news was communicated to Petipa (himself already a very old man) during a rehearsal. All he said was: 'Ah? We must die once!' and continued the rehearsal.

Johannsen taught until the year of his death. His wife died one month before him and this was to him a terrible blow. His life-long companion in the flesh, he

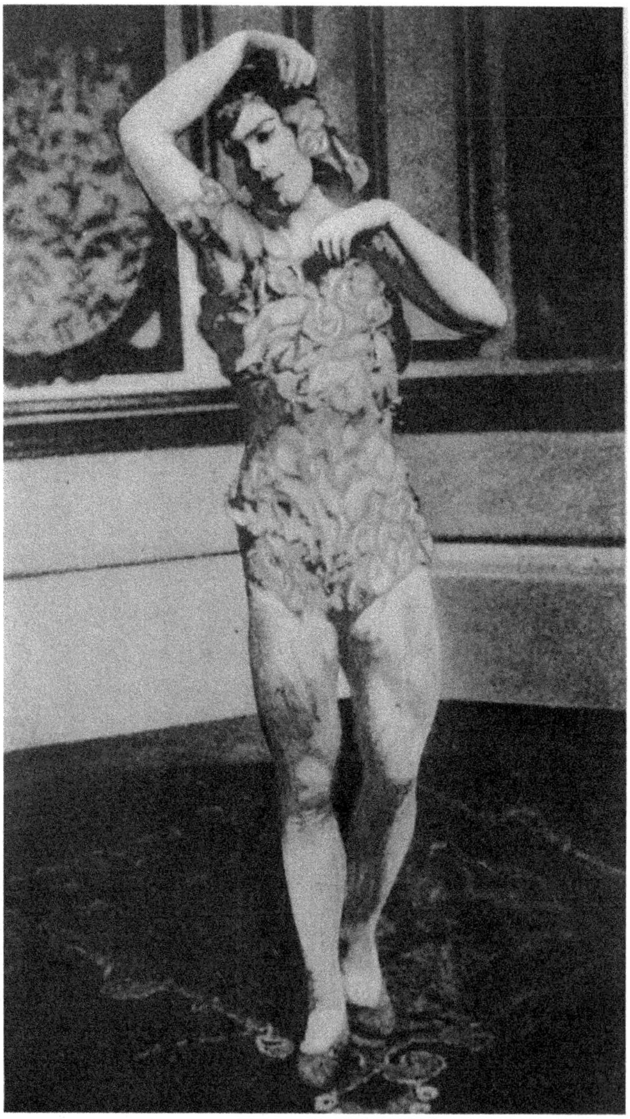

Nijinsky, Spectre de la Rose

could not bear being parted from her for a moment even in death, and at night he stole into the chamber where she lay to fondle her cold face. Coming out he struck his head against the doorpost and brought on a stroke of paralysis. I shall never forget calling on him next day. The stroke had in some way affected his vocal organs and he was unable to speak. He seized his chin with his hand and worked it angrily up and down to indicate the misfortune that had come upon him. Within a month he followed his wife to the grave, and thus there passed away the Grand Old Man of the dance, a giant in his art, who elevated the technique of the ballet to superhuman levels, and imbued it with the dignity of a religion.

Nijinsky, Tricorne

CHAPTER THREE

THE MAKING OF A DANCER AND BALLET MASTER

The physical training which all aspirants to eminence in the ballet were put through at the Theatre School was very severe. The pupils were vowed to the service of Terpsichore, and to this service all other things, including sometimes the interests of general education, were sacrificed. The 'bad boys' of the school were forgiven everything if only they were good artists, and my own Theatre School memories are profusely interspersed with schoolboy pranks, subterfuges to escape the penalties of unlearned lessons, and tricks played on teachers. Our geography teacher was enamoured of Zucchi, and a good three-quarters of every geography lesson was taken up (at our initiative) with eulogies of Zucchi's incomparable charms. Our German teacher was short-sighted and paid dearly for this defect. My keenest recollection of him is with a stream of ink trickling down his cheek from an inkpot I had concealed in his hat. Let it be frankly admitted that I was a thoroughly bad boy and never learnt my lessons, but, armed with a Didelot scholarship, I passed through school with the ease of a launched vessel gliding into the waiting waters.

But impatience with imposed book-lore was but a measure of my eagerness to reach the dancing class room or gymnasium. Every moment of free time was occupied in either dancing or studying others dance, or in music (I played the piano, the violin, and the balalaika), or in wrestling, boxing, gymnastics, or some form of sport that improved the muscles and developed the physique. In all these occupations my inseparable companion was my younger brother Serge, who, had he not died a tragic death at an early age, would surely have become one of the greatest dancers of all time. The dancing class room was to us a temple, and our attitude towards our art was as towards a religion.

Only by love and hard work can you become a good dancer—love of hard work and love of the art. Dancing is no art for the faint-hearted. Not a few were there, even in Russia, who, having put their hands to the plough, turned back. The school and the theatre were well rid of them. The sieve had a wide mesh. Only the greatest remained.

Discipline, merciless and unsparing discipline, was the secret of our success, and love of that discipline which triumphed over its pains. The hardest worker I ever knew was my father, Gustav Legat, and he set us a noble example. At the entrance examination to the Theatre School at the age of sixteen, his *adagio* caused astonishment, for his *developpé* was so advanced that no finished dancer could compare with it. To arrive at this result he had already worked upon himself as a lad for several years without missing a single day's work. He lived at Staraya Derevnia, a distance of four miles from the Theatre School. Rising early he would do his exercises in his bedroom. Then, quickly dressing, he walked (the family was very poor) to the school, always clad, even in the depths of winter, in the same light summer overcoat. Before the general class began he managed to get in some work alone, then did the class work together with the other pupils under the instruction of Marius Petipa. After class my father would still stay on and wait the arrival of Christian Johannsen, who came to do his own practice. With him my father would repeat the entire class. He never left the school until he was all but forced out, then once again did the four miles afoot home to Staraya Derevnia, again the exercises in his room, and only then sleep and repose. He always lay on his back, and to develop the turning out of his feet fixed them into the sides of his bed with the instep upwards. In this uncomfortable position he often slept till morning.

Not only did his feet turn outwards to a phenomenal degree, but his legs were astonishingly strong. He was able to lift his leg in a *developpé* with a boy sitting on his foot. Another feat he performed was to carry a glass full of water steadily balanced on the inside of his heel with his leg raised in a *developpé* of the second position. The outward development of his instep had its disadvantages, however. It resulted in a distinct loss of elevation, despite his muscular strength.

Christian Johannsen used to say to us: 'Work not only till the sweat comes, but till the blood comes through the pores of the skin—only then you'll be a dancer!' That was the spirit in which we learned to work, never sparing ourselves and always looking for knowledge from every available source.

When I was a boy I loved athletics. My brother Serge and I—the new Legat 'inseparables'—were members of athletic, gymnastic, and rowing clubs. We rowed, swam, did acrobatics and weightlifting, frequented the circuses, worked with the clowns and tumblers, wrestled, and, in addition to this, were painters, and musicians in a balalaika orchestra—all at the same time that we were working to become the two first dancers in the Imperial Ballet! It all helped—for one of the principles of the Russian school was rounded-out training. Provided the master-sculptor has the last word in your moulding, it matters not where you get your knowledge, or from whom, as long as you get it. But it requires years of work, work, work. I remembered old Johannsen's words, and used to examine my arms and hands when I was nearing exhaustion to see if the blood was actually coming through, as he said it ought!

My father, like Johannsen, was a severe teacher. He started teaching me when I was eight. He used to say: 'You'll never be a dancer, you'll play the violin, or become a painter.' My little legs worked mechanically, my little heart did not yet understand. But my father never lost hope. He went on drilling me.

Serge Legat

I worked with him till I was over twenty. He was merciless in his severity. My brother Serge worked with me. When we had held a *developpé* as long as we could, and still a bit, father would exclaim: 'Hold it still longer, you rascals!' And we did. It hurt, but we did it.

One day at the Theatre School, when I was still in the class of Paul Gerdt, the latter was setting a *pas de deux* for myself and Alexandra Vinogradova. He wanted her to leap into my arms in the flight called 'the fish.' She was afraid. Gerdt said: 'I'll show you.' He knew my strength. He took a leap several paces away, flew through the air and landed straight on my outspread arms, where I held him. He must have weighed about 170 pounds.

This strength stood me in good stead as a supporter. Our heaviest ballerinas were featherweight for me. Legnani was the most brilliant of the Italian dancers. Paul Gerdt was her first partner on the Marinsky stage, but one day he hurt his foot, and Petipa said: 'Let's see what Legat can do in his place.'

After that Legnani always had me as her partner, and for three years we worked together daily. Then Petipa began to allocate to me more and more important roles, and I danced in over fifty of his productions. In course of time I arrived at a position where I was practically able to dictate exactly what I would do or would not do.

Only by incessant work and untiring application were our dancers made. But our ballet masters were not made—they were born. Neither Christian Johannsen nor my father ever produced a ballet in their lives. On the other hand, Marius Petipa was a mediocre teacher, but a born choreographer. As choreographer he was my prototype, and I followed in his steps. From my youth up I observed closely not only how others danced, but also how dances were set and arranged. Once, shortly after I had graduated, there came a dancer from Moscow by name Masalova, who was a distant relation of mine, and who asked me to set for her a *pas de deux*. I was always fond of experimenting, so I accepted *the* invitation. *Pas de deux* had heretofore only been set to adagio in slow time. I broke this tradition, and with my very first experiment took a waltz. It was highly successful, and from that time onward waltzes for *pas de deux* became popular. The waltz became my favourite tempo for *pas de deux*, and I set a great many. One of the best known was the *Valse Caprice* to the music of Rubinstein, which I danced first with Olga Preobrazhenskaya.

I began to be in demand for setting *pas de deux, trois, quatre*. I discovered in myself an intuitive flair for the latent possibilities of individual dancers. I saw the differences in their relative capacities. I realized exactly in what poses, what movements, what groupings and combinations each would be shown up to the best advantage, having in view individual peculiarities. I sought to elicit and enhance virtues, I sought to mask defects. This was the secret of my success as a producer. I was never either iconoclast or pioneer of new forms. I was simply a seeker of beauty in individuals.

At Petipa's request I set a good many such *pas de deux, trios, quatre* in his later ballets. One day, shortly before his daughter, Lubov, was to make her début, Petipa said to me in his broken

Russian: 'I want big success. You dance with Lubov. You set dance.' The dear old man was so nervous about the event that he was afraid to set the dance himself. I was pretty nervous myself at being set such a task, in such a manner, by such an authority. But when it was over Petipa embraced me and said:' Da, ya vizh ti mozh karasha komposi!' ('Yes, I see thou able good compose!')

A short time after this, Paul Gerdt asked me to set the dance for the final examination of his godchild, Tamara Karsavina. He not unnaturally regarded her with especial favour, and was anxious that her first important appearance should be a signal success. I chose for her a *pas de deux* from the ballet *Svoenravnaya Zhena* (*The Wilful Wife*). Drigo accompanied and conducted at the performance. Gerdt set the dances of his pupils himself, but, like Petipa, he said he feared such a responsibility in the case of a relative. Tamara's partner was to be Theodor Kozloff, who was also graduating, and had been sent from Moscow to complete his training in the senior class under my tuition. Kozloff was one of my best pupils, and I accepted the invitation with pleasure. I set them a very simple but effective *pas de deux* designed to show up Tamara's many natural graces to the maximum of advantage. The dance was an overwhelming success and Karsavina was magnificent. She and Kozloff stood out among all the other participants. Her father (himself an excellent dancer and teacher) and her godfather thanked me profusely.

Recently, on a visit to London from America, where he has made a big name for himself both on the stage and the screen, Theodor Kozloff recalled this incident. 'Neither Tamara nor I would have got anywhere without you,' he said. It is pleasant to have one's old pupils thus show their appreciation.

This ability to judge of the performer's capacities and show them off to the best advantage is a sort of special sense, very subtle, and not to be acquired by learning. If you haven't got it by nature, you are unlikely ever to acquire it. Both my brother and I possessed it, although it never manifested itself in my father.

My brother Serge was now becoming a prominent dancer, and as everything we did we did together, we began to exercise our imagination in collaborating in the setting of dances. One day the director informed me that it had been decided to invite us to produce a new ballet, *The Fairy Doll,* at the Hermitage Theatre of the Winter Palace for a special performance at which the Tsar was to be present. This remarkable invitation confused me at first, for it was naturally expected that only Petipa would be asked to produce at this, the private theatre of the Tsar, and on this ground I saw fit to beg to be excused. But I was told that my creations on the Marinsky stage had attracted very favourable attention, and it was the order of the director, M. Teliakovsky, that I should produce on this occasion. My brother and I, dancing the two pierrots with the doll Matilda Kshesinskaya, set the ballet together, doing alternately eight bars at a time. It met with great success, and the Tsar chose it for a performance at the Marinsky Theatre when he was going to bring his children to the ballet for the first time. Alas, I was unable to appear at this performance, for I had an accident which left me on crutches for three months. I delegated my role to Michel Fokine, then one of my best pupils in the senior class, and there was a furore when Serge and Fokine led me out on the stage on crutches.

There were other ballet masters in the Imperial Theatre at this time, but all were overshadowed by the titanic Petipa. Nevertheless, some good ballets were produced by Lev Ivanoff and Gorsky. One or two Italians, including Cecchetti, also tried their hand at producing, but proved to be better dancers than choreographers. Petipa it was who dominated the choreographic world, who laid the choreographic structure to the Russian ballet, and upon the foundations he established all the later choreographers, Fokine, Romanoff, and others of marked originality and imagination, built.

The ideal ballet master must have a keen sense of beauty, of groupings, and of the capacities and peculiarities of his artists. He must also have a quick eye and a ready imagination. Perrot, the French ballet master, who preceded the Petipas, had everything but the quick eye and the

N. Bergner. Engineer of the Marinsky Theatre, St. Petersbourg and a pioneer of modern stage craft

ready imagination, and thus failed. He took two years to produce one ballet! He would sit in a circle of silent artists, thinking. The music would be played. He would think again. The music would be played again. Another silence. Then he would send them all home for the day—the muse hadn't yet inspired him! When he did get inspired the result was beautiful, but what a time it took!

Since Petipa's time there have been many new tendencies in ballet, 'iconoclast,' 'modern,' and vague tendencies back to 'nature.' Some of these tendencies represent valuable and permanent developments in the art, others I regard merely as passing freaks. For iconoclast, orthodox, or modern, every aspiring ballet master is doomed ultimately to failure who prefers the grotesque to the graceful, and who ignores the principle that the secret of beauty lies in simplicity.

CHAPTER FOUR

THEATRICAL MEMORIES

A potent factor in the building up of the Imperial Ballet was the disciplinary system that reigned in the Imperial theatres. If, at the Theatre School, examiners looked through their fingers at the scholastic shortcomings of promising Terpsichorean devotees, no such leniency awaited them once they had blossomed forth either as members of the *corps de ballet* or to the ranks of the junior soloists.

Woe betide a member of the company who appeared thirty seconds late for rehearsal, or whose practice dress showed the slightest deviation from the ordained standard, or whose *battements* were out of tempo and suggested undue nocturnal gaiety or vigil! We were drilled with all the severity of a military machine; yet was there no danger of mechanical automatism in our work, for this discipline applied to the company as a whole, while in the class room each pupil separately was the object of the eagle eye of Johannsen and his associates, seeking individual beauty as well as collective effect.

As members of the Imperial Ballet Company we belonged to the State, or rather, personally to the Emperor. We were his servants, his employees, as an aesthetic institution we were his property. In our lives we were guarded and favoured in many ways with the aim of concentrating our specialization as dancers. To some extent we were a hot-house product. This may not always have promoted our wider individual development as members of a community or a nation, and not many were there among the ballet company who, like my brother and myself, were also professional musicians and painters, broadening our training by a large diversity of parallel interests and occupations. Yet it was this protected specialization which was the secret of the collective artistic purity and perfection of the Imperial Ballet, and which made of it, as a unit, a thing of beauty never before and probably never again to be seen.

Thus a slip on the stage, a noticeable fault in execution, was not only a personal defect, it was an offence against the institution and was penalized as such. Only once was I ever fined for malexecution, and though I paid the penalty, I may in all conscience say it was really not my fault, but my partner's, as she admitted. I was dancing with Anna Johannsen, our old professor's daughter. At the conclusion of our *pas de deux* we had to separate towards each end of the stage and execute a pirouette.

At the conclusion of my pirouette I saw Anna at the other side of the stage on the floor, and I was subsequently charged with having allowed her to fall. When I was informed of the penalty I defended myself on the ground that I had performed the dance as set by Petipa, and that anyway I couldn't have stopped Anna from falling unless I had an arm twenty feet long. But I was fined ten roubles all the same. Technically the male partner is responsible for the support of his lady in all circumstances, and I was supposed to have foreseen her accident and prevented it.

Once I really did let my partner fall, and by my own fault, yet, oddly enough, this incident passed without penalty. It was in *Tsar Candaule,* when I was still a very young dancer. I had to adopt a sitting posture at the base of a statue with one foot stretched forward, and thus await my partner, who should throw herself into my arms. By inadvertence or nervousness I put the wrong foot forward, and consequently had not the same balance with which to support the lady when she arrived in my arms The ballerina was Varvara Nikitina, and I expected when she picked herself up that she would blame me bitterly. I stood before her full of confusion. But all she said was: 'No matter, my dear, let's go on,' and we ended the dance

Ladies of the Marinsky Theatre Ballet Company, early 1900

well. Behind the scenes I burst into tears with shame and apologies. But she was not angry, she took my head in her hands and kissed me, and this touching kindness left an indelible impression on me. Varvara Nikitina was not only a wonderful dancer, she was also a wonderful woman.

I mention these little incidents because young dancers, nervous and self-conscious, are inclined to think they alone are the victims of stage accidents. Let them take heart. We were all nervous once and we all made mistakes. I believe you have an English saying that a man who never makes mistakes never makes anything. A baptism of mishap, provided it is not serious, is as salutary for a dancer as a baptism of fire for a soldier. Even the strongest or most highly trained are not immune from accidents. Anna Pavlova was once dropped by Paul Gerdt in *Flora's Awakening.* At the point where she was supposed to fall into his arms he tripped on some object carelessly left lying on the stage, and fell on top of her. Enrico Cecchetti, on the occasion of his début in Petrograd, missed a pirouette and 'came a cropper' at the conclusion of his solo. But he picked himself up, and when he took his bow he turned a brilliant spin of pirouettes to make up for it.

You can hardly be inspired by mistakes, whether your own or anyone else's, but you may be inspired by the way others conquer misfortunes. When she was quite a young pupil of mine, Nadine Nicolaeva, who was later to become my wife, dancing at the Narodny Dom at Petrograd, had to appear after a scene in which a fountain had played on the stage. In the haste of changing scenes the floor had not been properly dried. Nadine completed a leap on a slippery place, turned somersault, and landed on her face. When she picked herself up blood was trickling both from her face and her right leg. Still she finished the dance amid cheers from the audience. But this applause was nothing to the ovation when she appeared again three minutes later and danced a difficult tarantelle from start to finish with undiminished brilliance.

In the course of more than thirty years' work on the stage I have encountered many strange experiences, but probably the strangest of all was when in the middle of a *pas de deux* I had a row of teeth knocked out at a single blow by my partner. I was dancing with the ballerina Olga Preobrazhenskaya at a charity performance at the Mihailoff Theatre. The audience consisted of the élite of the old Russian aristocracy. We were doing my *Valse Caprice* to the music of Rubinstein, and I had just set my partner off in a spin of pirouettes when she accidentally raised her arm and caught me in the mouth with the full force of her elbow. I felt the blood spurt in my mouth with a horrible gush, but I had sufficient presence of mind to close my lips tightly and support my partner, so that she finished her brilliant movement in a graceful pose. In the enthusiasm of the movement she was quite unconscious of what she had done, and, as for me, I would have rather died than show it. So I finished the dance, including my solo, and managed to appear for two or three bows without anyone suspecting what had occurred. But when at the insistent applause Preobrazhenskaya pulled me by the arm and said: 'We shall have to give an encore,' I could not hold out longer! I was obliged to open my mouth, and for answer spat four teeth out on the floor. Poor Olga swooned on the spot and was unable to continue the performance. For days she was full of heart-rending laments. I tried to make light of it, and many times after danced with her with no less pleasure and success than before.

But it's an ill wind that blows nobody any good. Lots of children (including many grown-up ones, too!) would have missed a hearty laugh at the grimaces I make with my removable teeth had Preobrazhenskaya not knocked out those that father and mother provided me with.

I had one other serious accident on the stage. I was dancing with Claudia Kulichevskaya in *Pharaoh's Daughter*. The whole of the ballet went splendidly until the last act. Here, at the commencement of a *pas de deux* with my partner, all of a sudden I seemed to hear beneath my left foot a crunching sound. I thought I had trodden on a nutshell or some other object dropped on the stage, and was about to step aside, when to my astonishment I found the foot no longer responded! The foot gave way beneath me, and horrified to find myself a cripple, I hobbled off the stage on the other foot. It appeared that with the last movement of my solo I had torn a tendon in the ankle. Matilda Kshesinskaya sent me home in her carriage, and Prince Volkonsky, director of the Imperial Theatres, sent his Swedish masseur to tend me. For three months I was on crutches, and was able to dance again only six months later. When I appeared in the theatre on crutches everyone crowded round in sympathy, and the dear old Italian regisseur, Coppini, burst into tears. A similar accident to this one happened to that wonderful character dancer, Bekefy.

Once, even after I had been fifteen years on the stage, I suffered a sort of sudden loss of memory immediately before my solo. The whole dance became an utter blank to me—I no longer had the faintest idea how it should start! But even in this extraordinary predicament I did not allow myself to lose self-possession. Vaguely I recalled that my solo began in the centre of the stage. I walked there and stood awaiting the conductor's signal. I cannot describe what ensued otherwise than to say that I 'awoke' in the middle of my dance. My whole body danced itself, and 'I,' so to speak, awoke to it only when the dance was half over! It is miraculous what secrets of power lie stored in the trained members of our body. Legnani told me she once had a similar experience.

This discipline of experience is still more valuable than the discipline of authority to which we are subjected, and of which I have already spoken. As for this latter, a few of us achieved positions where, in the end, we could (and did) practically dictate to the Director of the Imperial Theatres what we should do, or not do, in which ballets we should appear, and in which we shouldn't (that is, wouldn't). Among the men dancers of my time I alone was in this enviable position, but among the ballerinas there were two who were able to do the same. They were Matilda Kshesinskaya and, later, Anna Pavlova.

This, the most brilliant period of my career, is closely associated in my mind with my late brother Serge, who, I am convinced, had he lived, would have been one of the greatest artists of all time. Not only did we undertake many daring feats together, loving a joke and both being full of mischief, but we were jealous of the

Nicolas Legat with his wife, Nicolaeva

Anna Pavlova in “The Swan”

honour of our fellow-artists, and especially our ballet colleagues, and though we sometimes played with fire, we knew our worth and gambled with it. For instance, on the occasion when our composition, *The Fairy Doll,* had been produced by Imperial command at the Hermitage Theatre, our ballet formed the last part of the programme, the first two parts being drama and opera. Well, after the performance a special supper was served for the artists, but when we arrived after concluding the programme, we found that the operatic and dramatic artists had supped before us and consumed the best of the viands. Serge and I were furious at such treatment of our companions who had given the principal part of the evening's performance, and I got up and publicly announced that 'such hospitality did not meet with my approval,' and I invited the entire ballet troupe to be my guests at a well-known restaurant, where I would see that everyone had his favourite dish. The *régisseur* Aistoff, who was with us, was terrified at this proposal, which he said was an insult to the Emperor, and tried to persuade us just to go off home quietly. But I lost patience and insisted on having my own way. At that moment Prince P., director of the Imperial household, entered. Angrily he declared that for such unpardonable insolence Legat must be immediately dismissed from the Imperial Ballet. But at this Aistoff stood up for me and answered that directors of even Imperial households were to be had by the dozen, but Legats couldn't be picked off trees like apples! While they were disputing, my companions and I put on our things and made off, and I gave the whole company a hilarious banquet which lasted till the small hours of the morning.

I was a bit frightened by my action all the same. From the formal point of view, of course, my behaviour had been the last word in insubordination. So when I got home I thought it better to call up Matilda Kshesinskaya, who was at that time taking lessons from me and was a great friend of mine, and consult her about it. She promised as soon as she saw the Grand Duke Vladimir Alexandrovitch (who had been sent by the Tsar to congratulate us on our production) to transmit my apologies and intercede on my behalf. Next day Kshesinskaya said she had seen the Grand Duke, and that I need fear no penalties. Not only that, but I was promised that at the next Imperial performance at the Winter Palace the supper would be a thoroughly good one! And so it turned out! After the next performance, a few days later, a luxurious table was spread specially for the members of the ballet, and it was with loud hurrahs that we drank the toast to the Tsar!

The late Emperor was always very kindly disposed to me, and used to call me his 'double' because I had a talent for making-up and could make myself indistinguishable from him at a few paces' distance. I received many presents from him, and I knew I could always count on his gracious patronage if I got into difficulties. And I used the power of my position on more than one occasion, though I can honestly say I never once used it for myself alone, but always on behalf of my colleagues as well. I will narrate a practical joke my brother and I played on the stage during a public performance with the object of freeing ourselves and six of our colleagues from an unwelcome engagement. It was such a good joke that I consider it was worth while for its own sake, anyway, quite apart from its aim.

When Prince S. M. Wolkonsky was appointed Director of the Imperial Theatres he set himself the task of raising the standard of opera ballets by having ballerinas and premiers danseurs appear in them instead of second-line dancers as heretofore. The result was that I and my brother Serge found ourselves with twice as much work to do, dancing not only on the regular ballet evenings, but also in the operas, which we didn't like at all, regarding (in our youthful conceit) all opera ballets as a sort of surrogate of the 'real' thing. So I went to Prince Wolkonsky and protested on behalf of us all against being thus 'exploited.' But he replied that he was determined to raise the standard of the opera, and ordered us to go on appearing. But we were really fed up, and made up our minds to get out of it at all costs. And this is how we did it.

In the last act of the opera *Freischütz* there is a dance for four couples. For the four ladies' parts Wolkonsky appointed the ballerinas Anna Pavlova, Olga Preobrazhenskaya, Julia Sedova, and Vera Trefilova; and their partners were to be Gerdt, Bekefy, my brother Serge, and myself. All four of us wore exactly similar costumes. One night, when this opera had been given a bit too often for our liking, without saying a word to anyone, Serge and I made up our faces in exact replica of Bekefy, and lo, when we all four came out on the stage there was Gerdt and *three* Bekefys! The confusion that arose on the stage was indescribable, for Bekefy, Serge, and myself were the same height, so it was quite impossible for the ballerinas to distinguish one of us from the other, and they couldn't for the life of them tell who was their partner! The house rocked with laughter and shouted 'Bekefy!' Delighted, Bekefy hastened to acknowledge the applause, but like a shot Serge and I were at his side, all of us bowing Bekefys! The performance was held up, so great was the sensation, and I saw the Grand Duke Sergei Mihailovitch splitting his sides in a corner of his box.

Next day I was called by Prince Wolkonsky, severely reprimanded, and threatened with all sorts of disciplinary measures if we made any more fuss about dancing in operas. But I knew he couldn't do without us in the regular ballet performances, and I also knew our trick had been a success, and I boldly replied that unless we were relieved of the unwelcome work at the next performance of that opera there would appear not three Bekefys but four Gerdts! And the result of my ultimatum was a complete—and, let me add, very good-natured—capitulation on the part of the charming director.

I once played a similar trick on A. A. Gorsky, *maître de ballet* of the Moscow Grand Theatre. He was invited to St. Petersburg to reproduce the ballet, *The Hunchbacked Horse,* originally created by Marius Petipa, for the annual benefit performance of the *corps de ballet.*

Gorsky had a long beard and a very long moustache that drooped either side in Oriental fashion. My role in the ballet was that of the Khan's chief counsellor. The costumes and scenery had been designed by K. A. Korovine, and when I was discussing with him the question of my make-up I suggested, quite in fun, that I should make myself up exactly like Gorsky. Whether Korovine thought I was serious or not I don't know, but he

Leopold Auer

laughingly said, 'All right.' At the performance nobody recognized me as Legat, so exactly had I imitated the appearance of Gorsky, and when at the conclusion of the performance Gorsky was called out to the front with all the other artists the centre of the stage was occupied by two Gorskys, one an Oriental prince, the other in evening dress! Gorsky was a little piqued by the laughter of the audience, but we were friends from childhood days, and a bottle or two of champagne soon set things right.

My father once also got himself out of some unwelcome work by using a trick he knew with his feet. In a previous chapter I mentioned his phenomenal ability to turn his feet outwards. He was able to turn his feet out considerably further than the first position, in fact he could actually turn them backwards.

In the opera *Ruslan and Ludmilla* he was appointed to dance a Caucasian folk-dance, Lezghinka. Being purely classical in style, my father considered that others would dance this character number just as well as he, if not better. The director, however, insisted. But my father 'got his own back' in the following way. In the dance in question the men dancers hold one arm bent before their face, and thus only the legs and feet of the next figures in front are visible to them. Behind my father was a young man who knew the dance badly, and who, with his eyes fixed on my father's feet, was endeavouring to follow his exact movements. When the dance opened the whole line had to walk around the stage led by my father, while a few bars later they had to turn suddenly and move in the contrary direction. My father moved forward for two or three bars, and then all at once turned his feet so far outwards that they pointed backwards although he himself continued going forwards. The young novice behind, with his eyes glued to my father's feet, thought that my father had turned right about! He twisted round abruptly, the others in line followed suit, and the line was quite upset, and left my father moving across the stage alone with his feet pointing backwards!

My father was hauled over the coals for this incident, but Petipa and Johannsen both stood up for him. It was not Legat, they said, who turned at the wrong moment, but the others, and if Legat's feet turned well outwards, as became a classical dancer, then he should be praised for it, not blamed! After this affair my father was taken out of the opera, for which he was very grateful.

I have mentioned that my brother and I were very fond of drawing. Our room was covered with all sorts of sketches. Our tastes lay in the direction of the grotesque, and one day we suddenly thought of trying our hand at caricatures. First Serge had a go at me, and hit off the comic traits of my head very successfully. I followed suit and made a very funny drawing of him. Next we went at our colleagues in the theatre, and from that day became recognized cartoonists.

One day we showed a few cartoons at the opera, and Stravinsky (father of Igor) urged us to publish an album, to which he would be the first subscriber. We followed his advice and published a collection done in water colours. The album contained ninety-four cartoons of the most famous people of the day in the ballet world. It was published at twenty-five roubles, but in spite of this high price it was quickly sold out. A copy bound in white leather was presented to the Tsar Nicolas II. The title was *The Russian Ballet in Caricature,* by the brothers Nicolas and Serge Legat.

In view of this success we resolved to issue another large edition at our own expense. Having collected the money we made arrangements with a publisher, who, when he had printed about forty, decamped with both money and pictures, and we never saw him again! We had to recommence with another firm, and on the whole deal we lost about seven thousand roubles!

Then the artist P. A. Bergholtz induced us to submit a few cartoons to the Imperial Society of Water-Colour Artists. The latter displayed them at their next exhibition, and fixed a price of a hundred roubles apiece. They were bought out the very first day, several of them being purchased by the Grand Duke Vladimir Alexandrovitch, and from that time we became regular exhibitors of that Society, and we were made honorary members of it.

I lost everything I possessed in the Revolution, including my albums, but many people tell me the cartoons have great historical interest. All the originals are in the Bakhrushin Museum at Moscow, together with many others of our drawings, but I had the good fortune in London to find that my friend and former pupil, Laurent Novikoff, possessed a copy of our chief album in colours. By his courtesy I have had them all reproduced, and a selection of them appear in this book.

Serge was only twenty-eight when he died. All his life we had been inseparable companions, we held everything in common, we thought in common, we worked in common. I was his unfailing guide and preceptor, he never undertook anything without first consulting me, and he refused any offer in which I could not participate. But there was one side of his nature I was, alas, unable to control. He was highly imaginative and temperamental, and he conceived a mad and hopeless infatuation for a certain person associated with the ballet company. One day when I entered his room I found him lying on the floor with a razor in his hand. . . . He was already dead. . . .

Serge Diaghileff. Caricature by Nicolas Legat

CHAPTER FIVE

THE CLASS OF PERFECTION

In 1895, as an outcome of the improved technique of the growing generation of dancers and of the general development of the ballet, Christian Johannsen added a post-graduate class to the Imperial Ballet School. It was called the 'Class of Perfection,' and its object was to carry on the training of the best dancers after they had graduated from the Theatre School, and we were already appearing as artists on the Imperial stage.

When Johannsen confined his attention to the new class of perfection, I was appointed instructor to the senior boys' class of the Ballet School. The instructor of the senior girls' class was Paul Gerdt, and of the parallel girls' class, Enrico Cecchetti. The class of perfection was attended originally only by graduate women dancers, but Johannsen took into it my brother Serge and myself, and for a long time we were the only men in it. At that time, among prominent dancers in the class, were Anna Johannsen, Varvara Nikitina, Matilda Kshesinskaya, Julia Sedova, Olga Preobrazhenskaya, Marie Petipa (daughter of 'Marius'), and the youngest of all, Anna Pavlova.

The class was held in the large rehearsal hall next door to the Theatre School. The hall was about fifty feet square, well lighted and heated, and had a balcony. Its perfect floor, made of pine, was constructed with the same slight slope as the stage of the Marinsky Theatre. Mirrors ran the length of one wall, and the bars were fixed to the three others. All the walls were hung with portraits of great dancers and ballet masters, past and present. It was in every respect an ideal hall for ballet practice, and breathed an atmosphere all its own. In me it inspired a spirit of devotion. Each time I entered it I felt I was entering a temple—the same feeling I had towards the stage of the Marinsky Theatre.

The venerable Christian Johannsen's methods had the regularity of clockwork. He would appear in the class room a few minutes ahead of time, water the floor himself (to this he attached importance and was an adept at sprinkling it evenly), and see that all was ready for work. Then he would settle himself by the big mirror with his violin in his hand, and when the pupils were ready, curtly open the class with the minimum of civilities.

There were always more women than

Nicolas Legat. A self-caricature

men in the Class of Perfection. The men formed the back row, but Johannsen generally placed me in front of the class, as he used me for demonstration.

The tunes he played on his fiddle were either of his own composition or taken from old-time ballets. After his death his eldest daughter, Anna, presented me with his fiddle, saying, 'With this instrument my father taught you, your brother, your father, and many great artists. Take it now that he has passed his mantle on to you. There is no one he would so much desire should possess it as yourself.' I was very profoundly touched and treasured Johannsen's violin for years, until, with all my possessions, I lost it in the Revolution.

I have already described the old man's methods, his versatility, his ingenuity. They lasted until the day he retired. Then there was an interim of a few weeks, during which the former ballerina Evgenia Sokolova was given a trial as professor of the class. But Johannsen, who continued to supervise, was not satisfied, and told Mr. Teliakovsky, the Director of the Imperial Theatres, that he would prefer to try me in the job.

In one way it was no surprise to be told that I was to step into Johannsen's shoes, as he had often singled me out to demonstrate to the class. On the other hand, there was a great difference between unofficially deputizing and official appointment to the chair he had vacated. I felt the responsibility laid upon me to be enormous, and shrank before this official investiture. But the pupils I inherited from Johannsen were not only sympathetic and encouraging towards their new professor—they were something more. Already, the moment Johannsen had ceased to teach, many of them had come and requested me to form an unofficial class, which I had done, generally practising myself at the head of it. My official appointment therefore appeared to cause nothing but general satisfaction, although I was much younger than other instructors of the ballet school.

I have said that stage and class room were my temple. Let it not be thought, however, that our exercises were performed in an atmosphere of solemnity. It seems to me that any religion that makes you sad instead of joyful cannot be worth much, and we gathered in an atmosphere of gaiety. I always sought to lighten the burden of strenuous exercises by timely jokes and lively music. I enjoyed teaching, and I ardently desired my pupils to enjoy learning.

At the first few lessons Johannsen sat by my side. Extreme age could not dampen his ardour for his life-work nor his desire to see it worthily continued. At the age of over ninety his sight began to fail him, his vision narrowed, he could see clearly only what was straight ahead of him, and was obliged to turn his head to follow the object he wished to see. I felt there was something profoundly impressive, something tragic, in the situation: this old, old professor sitting beside me, his chosen pupil, more than sixty years his junior, transmitting to me his wisdom, anxiously guiding my every act, jealously following my every word, my every command. 'Enough of that movement,' he would say, 'now give them this one, . . . ' and so on. I was intensely nervous with the nervousness of reverence. To me the old man was the deity of the

Anna Pavlova, by Nicolas Legat

dance. With all my heart and all my soul I desired to hear his blessing: 'Well done, good and faithful servant.'

But Christian Johannsen rarely said as much as that at a time. His highest praise usually was, 'Now you may perform in public.' So when at the end of the first class he said to me: 'Good. You can go on,' I knew I had justified his hopes. He came to two or three more classes, but his corrections and comments became fewer and fewer. At his last visit he sat in silence. Only at the end he grunted 'Good.' And I know that when he died a few months later he died satisfied.

The Class of Perfection assembled every morning at 10.30. I followed Johannsen's example, and always arrived five minutes early to prepare the floor myself. Generally I donned a practice costume, consisting of a white shirt, black tights, tightly drawn up to the waist, and white dancing shoes, and in this costume demonstrated the steps I set at the head of the class. All being ready, I would call the pupils. The future ballerinas would enter like fairies, tripping lightly, impeccably attired in ballet-skirts of various hues, ethereally beautiful. After them would come the men dancers, bold and energetic, eager to bear their goddess-like partners skywards. I greeted every one of them separately-were they not all my friends as well as fellow-pupils? After stretching and warming up their legs, they took their places at the bar. I struck a chord on Johannsen's violin, and the class began.

Pliers, battements tendus, fondus, frappés, rond de jambe parterre et en l'air, developpés, grands battements, petits battements, port de bras—one after another the exercises followed each other, varied every day, while I closely followed each movement. 'In the centre, please! Adagio, *temps lié,* combinations of every kind, pirouettes and leaps, endless permutations and combinations, never the same twice, and finally the leaps and *tours en l' air* of the boys. . . . How indescribably beautiful it was to watch this group of budding virtuosos, all trained in the same school, and therefore all gracefully and silently moving in a perfect symphony of movement! Yet each had his or her particular quality, some secret charm or special ability to be brought out and developed. One had exceptional elevation, another unusual *ballon,* a third brilliant beats, a fourth wonderful *pointes,* a fifth remarkable *developpé,* and so forth. If they had difficulty in any particular steps or combinations, I would lay aside my violin and do the movements in front of them, and they would imitate.

Looking back, I see the class as if it were yesterday. Of every pupil I have some particular recollection. There, in the front row, is the inimitable Matilda Kshesinskaya, not only my pupil but also my close friend. Unequalled grace and brilliance were outstanding features of her dancing. How many glorious *pas de deux* we did together on the Marinsky stage, and how we took the Paris Grand Opera House by storm. And how delighted she was when, first of our Russian ballerinas, she did the famous thirty-two *fouettés.*

There, next to her, is Vera Trefilova, an exquisite piece of Dresden china come to life. She did not long remain in the class—she married and settled down to domestic life, never expecting to return to the stage. Long years passed. Then her husband died. She suffered a stroke and

Lydia Kyasht in "Javotte." Ballet arranged by Nicolas Legat

fell seriously ill. It appeared that one leg was partially paralysed. The prospect of dancing again seemed more remote than ever. So I was never so surprised as when one day, after the Revolution, she came to me in Petrograd and announced her wish to return to the stage. The problem was a delicate one. Many dancers think if they stop work for a prolonged period they will never be able to recommence. Much harm can be done by over-hasty action. The first day, despite her impatient tears, I permitted her to work a few minutes only. Next day a little more, and so on. The result was that, without a single complaint of sickness or pain, she regained in three months the technique it had taken years originally to acquire. She joined Diaghileff, reappearing on the Parisian stage in the same *Lac des Cygnes* in which, ten years before, she had danced with me at her 'farewell' performance, and her many admirers declared her art had in no wise suffered by the long interruption.

There, next to Trefilova, is Tamara Karsavina, exotic and beautiful, conquering all hearts by her penetrating charm. Next to her is Lydia Kyasht and Julia Sedova, Vaganova, Vil, and others. And there behind, amongst the boys, are Michel Fokine, Adolf Bolm, Vaczlav Nijinsky, Theodore Kozloff, Alexander Gavriloff.

Nijinsky was first brought to the Theatre School by his mother. The first impression he produced on the examining commission was an unfavourable one, for he appeared awkward in manner and delicate in health. But at the doctor's examination I was very struck by the formation of his thigh muscles. As instructor of the senior class, the last word as to the admission of candidates rested with me. I told Nijinsky to move a few paces away and jump. His leap was phenomenal. 'That youngster can be made into a fine dancer,' I said, and passed him without further ado. I had him put first into the junior boys' class under my brother Serge, but he made such rapid progress that I had him removed very soon to the senior class, and then to the Class of Perfection when I took this over from Johannsen. I set myself to develop those features in him which later distinguished him among all other dancers of his epoch—his phenomenal leap, his brilliant beats, his forceful *developpé*. He created a sensation upon his first appearance in the Marinsky Theatre, and it caused a sort of consternation when (very unjustly, to my mind!), as a result of breach of discipline, he was dismissed from the Imperial Ballet. Fortunately, Diaghileff took him, and he continued his studies under Cecchetti, and Europe saw more of this remarkable dancer than Russia ever did.

And many others there were, too numerous to mention, who in the course of ten years passed through my hands in the Class of Perfection. Several of them, besides working in the class, also studied with me privately. Anna Pavlova preferred to work in this way, and usually had her lessons on the stage of the Marinsky Theatre preceding rehearsals. She was thus properly warmed up and in the finest trim to rehearse. Sometimes I would don my practice costume and do the whole class with her. Then we were both in the finest fettle for rehearsal. Many, many ballets we danced together. Her favourite, *Giselle*, was also one of my favourites. My other favourite was *Esmeralda*, which Kshesinskaya usually danced with me.

Some of these pupils, such as Kozloff, received their early training in Moscow, and were sent to the St. Petersburg school for perfection. But Moscow also turned out some brilliant dancers without our aid, for the Moscow school also followed the principles laid down by Johannsen. Lydia Geiten, Lebedeva, Karpakova, Roslovleva, Katherine Geltzer (who to this day dances in Moscow), V. Tihomiroff, M. Mordkin, A. Volinine, and L. Novikoff were products of the Moscow school.

There was, however, much talent that remained in Russia and never became known beyond her borders. For instance, there was a Moscow dancer, Damashoff, who performed the most extraordinary feat I have ever witnessed. This man was of medium height, handsome, with very muscular legs. Having heard much about him, I went one day to watch him exercise. I still remember the gasp I gave when I saw him leap the first time. He seemed literally to remain high in the air and then slowly to descend. He did an *entrechat-huit* on the upward journey and descended with motionless legs. Then he reversed it, rising with motionless legs, and executing a complete *entrechat-huit* during the descent. Seeing my amazement, he said: 'Wait, I'll show you something.' Now the stage of the Moscow Grand Theatre is about twice as large as that of the Paris Opera or Covent Garden. Seating me on the edge of the director's box at the corner of the stage, Damashoff walked far away to the most distant corner, leaving the great empty space of the stage between us. I saw him take up a position, I saw him make a powerful movement, and to my unutterable amazement, flying like a bird, he was at my side in three leaps! Had anyone merely told me this is possible, I never would have believed it. Damashoff was a great dancer, but he never left Moscow. He was unknown not only abroad, but even in St. Petersburg, except by reputation.

Besides Nijinsky, Fokine also had good elevation, and of the previous generation Litavkin and Cecchetti both raised themselves like birds. But even Nijinsky's work was child's play compared with Damashoff.

I conducted the Class of Perfection until 1914, when I celebrated my jubilee of twenty-five years' service on the Imperial stage and took a prolonged leave to undertake a tour of Europe with Nadine Nicolaeva, who already presaged that wide development and daring enterprise which later made her excel, not only in classical, but also acrobatic and modern dancing. But our tour of that year was sadly disturbed by war's alarms. Before that I had had many invitations to leave Russia, but refused them all, making an exception only to appear with Kshesinskaya and Trefilova in Paris, and to do a European tour with Anna Pavlova in 1910. This latter was a very happy tour. We spent the days practising, the evenings performing, and the nights playing poker! When at the Opera Comique, Paris, Vera Trefilova and I were offered fifty thousand dollars a month if we would go to America, but Vera was about

Kira Nijinsky, by Nicolas Legat

to get married, and I was contracted to return to Russia. It was in the year of my tour with Pavlova that Diaghileff first approached me to join his newly formed company. But I occupied at that time simultaneously the three positions of first dancer and ballet master at the Marinsky Theatre, and director of the Class of Perfection; my salary was the highest ever paid in the history of the ballet; I felt my destiny inseparably linked with Russia, and I elected to remain there.

Perhaps, had I been able to see twelve years ahead, and had caught a vision of myself fleeing from the Bolsheviks with little but the clothes on my back, I might have chosen differently.

Forebodings of impending tragedy weighed upon me in January 1914, at my jubilee performance in the Marinsky Theatre. The Emperor Nicolas II and all his family were in the Imperial box. As fate would have it, it was not only my last appearance on my beloved Marinsky stage, it was also the Tsar's last visit to the Marinsky Theatre. A few months later the Great War broke out, followed by the still greater horrors of revolution. It was a terrible day for me when I heard of the brutal murder of the Emperor and all his family by the Bolsheviks.

I remember my strange heaviness of heart, even amidst the acclamations of the brilliant audience, on that occasion of my jubilee, and I attributed it at the time to my even temporarily parting from my beloved stage. But now I think, did my premonition lie deeper?

The enthusiasm of the evening was in no way affected thereby. With the inimitable Matilda Kshesinskaya I danced to perfection my favourite ballet *Esmeralda*, and at the conclusion, when all other presentations had been made, I received the Tsar's gift of a large gold cigar-case bearing the Imperial double eagle and a certificate conferring the title of 'Soloist of His Majesty,' accompanied by a pension for life—which, of course, I never drew.

The first years of this century marked the acme of development of the Imperial Ballet and the height of perfection of the Russian school of dancing. The history of the growth of both centres round the history of two men, Marius Petipa and Christian Johannsen. Learning and borrowing from everywhere, chiefly from French, Scandinavian, and Italians, they merged their gathered knowledge and experience, fermenting it with the genius of the Russian national character in the epoch of its florescence, and thus built up the eclectic system known as the Russian school.

Will ever again the possibility exist in allocating roles in a single theatre to select from such a list of artists: Matilda Kshesinskaya, Varvara Nikitina, Anna Johannsen, Kulichevskaya, Marie Anderson, Anna Pavlova, Olga Preobrazhenskaya, Julia Sedova, Tamara Karsavina, A. Vaganova, Lydia Kyasht, Lubov Egorova, Gerdt, Bekefy, Obukoff, Theodore Kozloff, Fokine, Nijinsky, Tikhomiroff, Mordkin, Volinine, Novikoff, Smoltzoff—to name but a few, for still the list is far from complete! This was the full bloom of the Russian Imperial Ballet, a height of general perfection never reached elsewhere than on the stage of the two principal Imperial Theatres, the Marinsky at St. Petersburg, and the Grand at Moscow.

Tamara Karsavina

Since I last danced in one of those theatres seventeen long years have passed, many of them in wanderings and exile. I look back and wonder. . . . Where are the happy days of the flowering of Russian art, fostered by a benevolent and beauty-loving monarch? Gone, as the sun obliterated by raging storms! Gone, like flowers withered in icy winds! Gone, with all the beauty of our Russian life!

And in place of high art and unself-seeking patronage, the world abounds in fungus growths and adventurers in art, pushing spurious wares, acquired by imitation at second or third hand, as if they were original and authorized goods!

Not in this day or in this age shall another such majestic artistic edifice arise as crumbled in the ruins of the Russian Revolution. But we, the product of that artistic culture, must give to other

A group of clever English pupils of the Legat School. Moira King, Barbara Vernon (who in 1937 won the World Championship for all classes of stage dancing, held in Paris), Joan Lendrum, Sandra Monteith (who won several medals in the 1937 Baby Championship, held in Paris), Elena Davidova and Villian Duncan

Legat taking advanced class. Amongst pupils are seen Phyllis Beddels and Stanley Judson

countries the benefit of that we know, and hand down the treasures we received. In the four quarters of the globe I behold the greatest dancers of my generation, many of them my pupils, upholding the standard of the great art, and if I am proud at the sight it is not merely a personal pride but a national pride, that we, in things material and political the despised and rejected of men, shall live for ever in thus transmitting a spark of the otherwise inexpressible soul of Russia. With this ideal I live, and with this ideal untarnished I shall die.

Anna Pavlova in "The Firefly"

APPENDIX 1

ANNA PAVLOVA

A Tribute

I remember Anna Pavlova when she was still quite a girl and had just entered the Imperial Theatre School. Slight of build, rather thin, with very expressive black eyes, she resembled a fairy more than a human being. From the first moment she manifested unusual talent. She also became very popular with her elders, whom she used to imitate and mimic cleverly, and in spare hours when the day's work was over she would attract attention by fantastic dances which she would invent for herself.

She received the title of 'ballerina' at an early age and created several roles that have become historic. In *Giselle,* which she first danced with me, she was both a charming peasant and a fascinating spirit. In *Bayaderka* she was the passionate dancing-girl, in *Don Quixote* the burning Spaniard, in *La Fille Mal Gardee* the naïve and simple country maid. She appeared to become the very incarnation of every part she played.

It was a serious loss to the Imperial stage when Anna Pavlova left Russia to make a name in western Europe. Thereafter her visits to Russia were of a temporary character, but upon every occasion she created a furore. She always asked me to dance with her on these return visits to her native country, and I also did a prolonged tour with her in 1910 in central Europe. She was an indefatigable worker and allowed no circumstance, however serious, to interfere with her daily work. I remember once when she had turned up for her class with me in the Marinsky Theatre she had forgotten all her practice clothes. Nothing daunted, she wrapped a couple of towels round her and did the whole class thus, indifferent to the stupid sniggering of stage-hands who happened to be in the theatre.

She was also perfect companion and friend. Never was heart so responsive, never spirit so overflowing with sympathy! Not only was she a great artist on the stage, but off the stage she was also a good and adorable woman. Caprice may be the prerogative of her sex, but her caprice knew no malice, but was rather the lively expression of impatience with everything unworthy, amateurish, hypocritical, artistically false. Anna Pavlova was a great dancer and a great woman, and the world is poorer and emptier for her loss. I loved her as an artist, colleague, and friend, and mourn in her the passing of the greatest product of the greatest age of Russian art.

Anna Pavlova in "The Swan." Courtesy of Walford Hyden

APPENDIX 2

LIST OF BALLETS IN WHICH NICOLAS LEGAT APPEARED

STUDENT PERIOD

Ballet	Produced by
Daughter of the Snows	Petipa
Pharaoh's Daughter	Petipa
Paquarette	Petipa
Mlada	Petipa
Rozana	Petipa
Night and Day	Petipa
The King's Orders	Petipa
Zaraya	Petipa
Deva Dunaya	Petipa

AS PRINCIPAL SOLOIST OR IN LEADING ROLE

Ballet	Produced by	Appeared with Ballerina
Gazelda	Perrot (renewed by Petipa)	M. Anderson
Zolushka	Petipa	P. Legnani
The Enchanted Forest	L. Ivanoff	M. Gorshenko
Pupils of Dupre	Petipa and L. Ivanoff	
Calcabrino	Petipa	C. Brianza

Ballet	Produced by	Appeared with Ballerina
Sylvia	Petipa	P. Legnani
L'Adventure de Damis	Petipa	O. Preobrazhenskaya
Golubaya Georgina	L. Ivanoff	M. Anderson
Waterman's Holiday	L. Ivanoff	V. Rikhliakova
The Wilful Wife	Perrot (renewed by Petipa)	M. Kshesinskaya
Sylphide	Petipa	V. Kulichevskaya
Vestalka	Petipa	
The Harlem Tulip	L. Ivanoff	
Le Marche de Paris	Petipa	
Love's Power	L. Ivanoff	V. Rikhliakova
Nymph and Satyr	L. Ivanoff (renewed by N. Legat)	A. Vinogradova
Catherine	Cecchetti	A. Nedremskaya
Paquita	Petipa	A. Johannsen and V. Kulichevskaya
Le Corsaire	Petipa	V. Rikhliakova
Bayaderka	Petipa	A. Johannsen, V. Kulichevskaya, Anna Pavlova, and N. Nicolaeva
The Magic Mirror	Petipa	M. Kshesinskaya
The Mikado's Daughter	L. Ivanoff	V. Rikhliakova
Blue Beard	N. Legat	
Fiametta	St. Leon (renewed by Petipa)	M. Kshesinskaya
Faust	Perrot (renewed by Petipa)	M. Kshesinskaya
Arlekinada	Petipa	O. Preobrazhenskaya and N. Nicolaeva
The Fairy Doll	N. and S. Legat	M. Kshesinskaya and V. Trefilova

Ballet	Produced by	Appeared with Ballerina
Le Roi Candaule	Petipa	M. Kshesinskaya, E. Vil, and V. Nikitina
La Source	St. Leon (renewed by Petipa)	A. Vaganova, O. Preobrazhenskaya, and V. Trefilova
Casse-Noisette	L. Petipa and Ivanoff	Delera, V. Trefilova, and O. Preobrazhenskaya
Kermess	N. Legat	O. Preobrazhenskaya
Caprice d'un Papillon	Petipa	O. Preobrazhenskaya, L. Roslovleva, and N. Nicolaeva
The Hump-backed Horse	Petipa	P. Legnani and M. Kshesinskaya
La Fille Mal Gardée	Petipa	Anna Pavlova, V. Trefilova, O. Preobrazhenskaya, and N. Nicolaeva
Giselle	St. Leon (renewed by Petipa)	H. Grimaldi, Anna Pavlova, N. Nicolaeva
Flora's Awakening	Petipa	O. Preobrazhenskaya
Talisman	N. Legat	M. Kshesinskaya
Raymonde	Petipa	O. Preobrazhenskaya and V. Trefilova
Don Quixote	Petipa	M. Kshesinskaya, Anna Pavlova, V. Trefilova, and O. Preobrazhenskaya
The Sleeping Beauty	Petipa	M. Kshesinskaya, J. Sedova, V. Trefilova, and O. Preobrazhenskaya

Ballet	Produced by	Appeared with Ballerina
The Lac des Cygnes	Petipa	Anna Pavlova, V. Trefilova, O. Preobrazhenskaya, and N. Nicolaeva
Coppelia	Petipa	Zambelli, M. Kshesinskaya, V. Trefilova, J. Sedova, E. Geltzer, O. Preobrazhenskaya, and N. Nicolaeva
Puss in Boots	N. Legat	M. Kshesinskaya
The Purple Flower	N. Legat	O. Preobrazhenskaya
Esmeralda	Petipa	M. Kshesinskaya
The Enchanted Flute	L. Ivanoff	A. Johannsen and N. Nicolaeva
Two Thieves	N. Legat	N. Nicolaeva
The White Lily	N. Legat	N. Nicolaeva and O. Preobrazhenskaya
The Rose of Margita	N. Legat	N. Nicolaeva
The Prince's Enchanted Dream	N. Legat	N. Nicolaeva

Nicolas Legat also appeared in several of these productions in various countries of Europe, and during the period when he was instructor to the company of Serge Diaghileff, took parts in *Carnaval, Petroushka,* and *La Boutique Fantasque.*

Dolin, by Nicolas Legat

APPENDIX 3

LIST OF BALLETS PRODUCED BY NICOLAS LEGAT

The Fairy Doll (first performance at Imperial Hermitage Theatre at royal command)

Blue Beard (for Jubilee of Paul Gerdt)

The Four Seasons (for Jubilee of Alexander Glazounoff)

Two Thieves

Puss in Boots

The Purple Flower

The Prince's Enchanted Dream

Rose of Margita

The White Lily

Kermess

Talisman

The Khan's Dream

La Chasse de Diane

Nymph and Satyr

Nicolas Legat also composed a very large number of dance items which were either performed separately or were incorporated in the ballets of other producers.

Porcelain statuette, by Pavlova

HERITAGE OF A BALLET MASTER

NICOLAS LEGAT

HERITAGE OF A BALLET MASTER

NICOLAS LEGAT

Compiled and edited by John Gregory
in collaboration with André Eglevsky

The Brothers Legat. Painted caricature.

THE AUTHORS' THANKS are due to all the contributors who have given freely of their time and thought to assist in making this book possible, and to Vera Krasovskaya, author of *Russian Ballet Theatre of the 20th Century*, and the late Fedor Lopukov, author of *Forty Years in Ballet*, for permission to quote; also to Patrick Hall for permission to publish the Class Music.

The authors would like to express their further thanks to Leda Anchutina, Nicholas Beriosoff, The British Council (Eastern Department), Mary Clarke of the *Dancing Times*, Natalya Dudinskaya, Ivor Guest, Baird and Lily Hastings, Judyth Knight, Vladimir Koshevnikoff, the Leningrad Choreographic School and Museum, Anna Legat-Pinness, Tatiana Legat, Dr. Llewellyn Smith, British Cultural Attaché in Moscow, the Ministry of Culture of the U.S.S.R. and the Central Archives Moscow, the late Natalya Roslavleva, Doris Sonne, and Alexander Ukladnikov for their advice and assistance in giving access to records, papers, photographs, programs and information.

Foreword

WHEN I ARRIVED IN LONDON for the first time with the Diaghilev Ballet I was thrilled because here was the teacher of my teacher, Madame Vaganova, and now I could study with this real master, Nicolas Legat. He was quick witted, a capable painter, a good pianist. Mr. Legat was delightful, and most lovable. He was a tireless teacher. The variety of movements he taught was enormous. Leonide Massine told me how much Mr. Legat helped him, as well as many other dancers.

Whenever I was in London, I studied regularly with Mr. Legat. In Paris, I studied with Madame Egorova.

We dancers always know when we have had "a good class"—when we want more! With Mr. Legat I always wanted more. For me personally, the way he helped my beats and turns was invaluable. Mr. Legat knew how to warm up a dancer's body by the right exercises. He would make the body limber and able to move better, faster, and to jump higher. When he saw, so rightly, that my extension was not enough, he found the very exercise I needed to improve it. He saw at once what we needed, and he pushed us forward, always forward. He was right when he said, "Unless you progress, you regress."

Alexandra Danilova

Nicolas Legat, Alexandra Danilova and André Eglevsky in the Baron's Court studio, London 1936.

PART I

NICOLAS LEGAT: 1869-1937

A Remembrance of Nicolas Legat

I WAS FIFTEEN YEARS OLD and a member of the de Basil Ballet Russe when I first came to London in 1933. During the long season at the Alhambra Theatre, Leonide Massine, our artistic director, arranged for a small group of the dancers to take classes with the renowned teacher Nicolas Legat. I was one of the group, together with Alexandra Danilova, and Massine himself, who was perhaps the most ardent student of us all.

Monsieur Legat was small of stature, slim and completely bald. He shaved what hair he had. He accompanied his classes seated at a grand piano, playing little tunes and chords of his own rhythmic phrasing. Many of his combinations were based on the count of five or seven, instead of the more conventional four or eight. He demonstrated the steps with his fingers on the lid of the piano, and we would crowd around him to catch his brief instructions. Returning to our places, we would go over the steps mentally. Legat rarely got up to demonstrate. If he did, it usually meant an inability on our part to grasp a step. This could put him in a furious mood, which we naturally tried to avoid, so we worked our brains full tilt. The master spoke very little English, and his few remarks were often sharp, but laced with wit. We were not dismayed by his piercing wit, or his devastating mimicry; after all, we had come to learn at any price, not to be praised.

Self-caricature of the Maestro.

Monsieur Legat noticed me at the first class I took with him but, not remembering my name, he called me "the boy with the red handkerchief," because of the handkerchief I wore to hold down my unruly hair. He began to take a special interest in me and he opened my eyes to the technical problems, to the artistry and expression of the classical dance, in a way I had never dreamed. During the few weeks that I came for lessons I absorbed so much that my friends and colleagues noticed a phenomenal progress in my work. The more I worked with Legat the more I realised the greatness of the man and the system. I began to make plans to study with him for a longer period, and this I was able to do the following summer. At the end of the season I left the Ballet Russe, giving up my position as soloist and sacrificing a good salary so that I could stay in London, without work or money, to be able to study continuously with the master.

Although I *pirouetted* well before studying with Legat, my turns were insecure—one day good, one day not so good—I could never guarantee my performance. It was Legat who taught me to control my balance during *pirouettes*. By the time I left Legat's studio and came to America, I was able to turn fifteen *pirouettes* without difficulty, a feat which helped me to win a bet with George Balanchine. At that time I was very hard-up, and to ensure that I would be able to buy my lunch, I used to wager Mr. Balanchine I would turn twelve *pirouettes* for him. I never went hungry.

Anticipating the time when I would leave London and no longer have the benefit of his guidance, I asked Nicolai Gustavovitch, as I addressed him, to give me a sample lesson which I could practice myself on tour. To my delight, one day I received from him an envelope containing four complete classes which he had written out in Russian with French terms. These written classes became my bible.

In 1936, I joined the Rene Blum - Michel Fokine Ballet Russe de Monte Carlo with which I toured Europe and South Africa. Towards the end of the year, on my return to London, I found Monsieur Legat seriously ill and unable to teach. His wife, Madame Nicolaeva-Legat, had taken over his classes. Every day I went to class with her, but before and afterwards I would sit by the bedside of Nicolai Gustavovitch and listen to his stories of fabulous dancers of other days: Johannson, Legnani, and Cecchetti. He was often carried away by the glorious memories of his dancing career and the great era of the Maryinsky. It was very inspiring for me. And he never failed to ask what I did in class, and would give me special steps on which to work.

I believe that the four lessons which Nicolas Legat wrote out for me should be published. Unlike the Cecchetti system that of Legat is not widely known in the West. It is therefore important that this document, which contains something of the structure, the essence, and the style of all that is best in Russian Ballet, should be available to students and teachers throughout the world.

André Eglevsky

A Biographical Sketch

NICOLAS LEGAT WAS BORN in St. Petersburg on 27 December 1869. The greater part of his life was spent in Russia, where he enjoyed a brilliant career as *premier danseur* at the Maryinsky Theatre, and as teacher of the Class of Perfection at the Imperial Theatre School. He was also a gifted musician, a sensitive choreographer, and his skill as a caricaturist was renowned.

Legat was a third generation dancer—his grandmother, Constance Lede, was a ballerina at the Paris Opéra, his father and mother were both dancers in the Bolshoi Ballet, Moscow. The Legats had come to Russia from Sweden during the reign of Nicolas I. It was said they came at the personal invitation of the Czar.

Nicolas and his brother Serge had their first ballet training from their father Gustav, who by all accounts was something of a martinet. In 1880, Nicolas was awarded a State (Didelot) Scholarship to the Imperial Theatre School, where he studied first under Professor Volkov. He graduated in 1888 and became a favorite pupil of Christian Johannson, the great Swedish teacher, under whose guidance the Maryinsky Ballet produced its finest dancers.

It is well known that Enrico Cecchetti came to Russia in 1887 and that the Russian dancers, including Legat, came under his spell. However, even though they absorbed considerable technical advances from Cecchetti's method, many of the Russian dancers preferred to keep the gracious "French" style and the scientific yet creative freedom of Johannson's method. Nicolas Legat was one of these.

In his memoirs Legat has written: "The secret of the development of Russian dancing lay in the fact that we learnt from everybody, and adapted what we learnt to ourselves. We copied, borrowed from, and emulated every source that gave us inspiration, and then, working on our acquired knowledge, and lending it the stamp of Russian national genius, we moulded it into the eclectic art of the Russian Ballet."[1]

According to Vera Krasovskaya: "As a dancer Legat's physique did not entirely measure up to the romantic stage personality of the 19th century. He was not tall, but stocky, with a rather large head. He had coarse features."[2] He was less handsomely endowed than his brother Serge, who died tragically in 1905. Fedor Lopukov writes of them: "They developed a wide range; Nicolai—lyrico-romantic, Sergei—lyrico-heroic. They amassed a huge repertoire from heavy romantic to buffo comico roles. All parts were easy for them. Nicolas developed many qualities, noticeably his very soft deep *plié.* His muscles and tendons were elongated, but his top half did not correspond to the lower part of his body—a Hercules too robust and too heavy for the Apollo-like structure of the legs."[3]

The talents of Nicolas were more suitable to those of the *demi-caractère* dancer, but his elegance and academic training enabled him to shine in romantic parts. He was an outstanding partner—strong and agile. He could lift 150 pounds dead weight, and at the same time be sensitive and unassuming. Ballerinas who danced with him could not help expressing the pleasure they experienced in being partnered by him; consequently he was much sought after by the leading ballerinas of the day: Legnani, Kschesinska, Pavlova, Preobrajenska and Treflova.

"There was a branch [of ballet]," writes Vera Krasovskaya, "in which the histrionic flair of Legat opened to the full; not in hero-lover parts, but in lover-simpleton parts, where romanticism was colored by humor, and lyricism was blended with comedy and pathos." She quotes from the memoir of I.F. Kschesinsky, a colleague: "Nicolai was superb in the technical sense as a classical dancer, and excelled as a partner, and yet one must say, if he had followed his vocation, he ought to have chosen the career of comic."

In his choreographic development, Legat was to a large extent nurtured and moulded by his teacher Johannson, and by the choreographer Petipa. Petipa looked upon Legat as a disciple who was extending his ideas. He trusted him to create many male variations, for which he, Petipa, had no great skill. Petipa was delighted when some of Legat's innovations brought him laurels, but when he realised that his apprentice was becoming a rival, his enthusiasm cooled.

The Legat brothers' greatest triumph was reached with their first choreographic work, *The Fairy Doll*, to music of Joseph Bayer in 1903. This piece broke away from the rigid classicism and the mythical fairy tale content of Petipa's ballets. It introduced human characters from the troubadour world and the circus, it had haunting waltzes, and it even contained a tap dance. The ballet enjoyed enormous success and hastened the retirement of Petipa as ballet master.

Though the Legat brothers contributed to a fresh trend in ballet at the turn of the century, they did not pursue the new or avant garde. Soon Serge was to pass from the scene and Nicolas appointed himself the guardian of tradition. By nature and upbringing a traditionalist, he vehemently opposed the re-

Caricature of the brothers Legat depicting their father, Gustav, putting them through their paces.

Above: Nicolas and Serge Legat with Olga Preobrajenska in their greatest choreographic success Fairy Doll.

Right: Detail from the program of the first performance of Fairy Doll *given at the Maryinsky Theatre, 16 February 1903.*

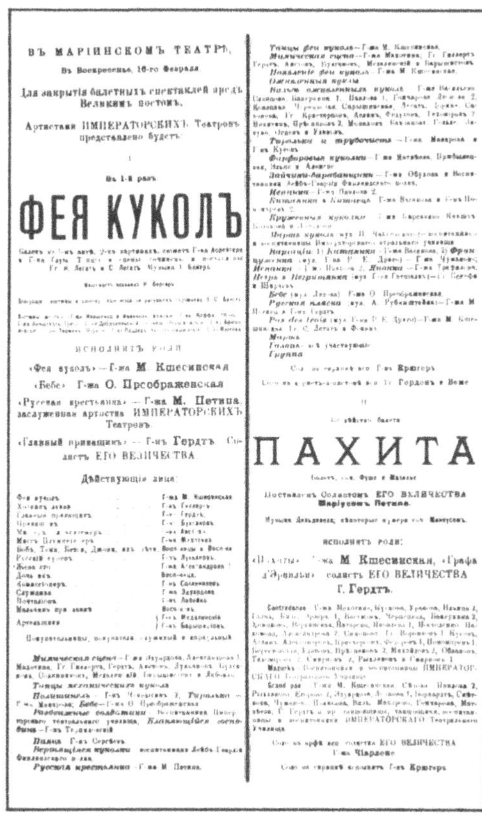

ВЪ МАРІИНСКОМЪ ТЕАТРѢ,

Въ Воскресенье, 16-го Февраля

Для закрытія балетныхъ спектаклей предъ Великимъ постомъ,

Артистами ИМПЕРАТОРСКИХЪ Театровъ представлено будетъ:

I

Въ 1-й разъ

ФЕЯ КУКОЛЪ

«Фея куколъ» — Г-жа М. Кшесинская

«Бебе» Г-жа О. Преображенская

«Русская крестьянка» — Г-жа М. Петипа, заслуженная артистка ИМПЕРАТОРСКИХЪ Театровъ

«Главный приказчикъ» — Г-нъ Гердтъ. Солистъ ЕГО ВЕЛИЧЕСТВА

Дѣйствующія лица:

II

ПАХИТА

Поставленъ Солистомъ ЕГО ВЕЛИЧЕСТВА Маріусомъ Петипа.

Исполнитъ роли:

«Пахиты» Г-жа М. Кшесинская, «Графа д'Эрвильи» солистъ ЕГО ВЕЛИЧЕСТВА Г. Гердтъ.

forms and modernism of Michel Fokine. There ensued a desperate conflict that brought unfortunate results, because the product of Legat's teaching was in essence the material of Fokine's choreography. They should have complemented each other with their work; instead their rivalry grew into a destructive war.

Legat began teaching early and taught in private houses before he was appointed an instructor in the Imperial Theatres. Soon after the death of Christian Johannson he was appointed his successor as master of the Class of Perfection. Many great artists passed through his hands including Nijinsky, Fokine, Bolm, Oboukhov, Leontiev, Preobrajenska, Kschesinska, Vaganova and Trefilova.

From the pen of Fedor Lopukov comes a concise appraisal of some of Legat's remarkable qualities:

> Legat's art was astonishing! Intuitively he knew what each pupil in the class required. When a movement was given to all present, he made one

Anna Pavlova and Nicolas Legat in Pas de Ruban from La Fille Mal Gardée.

correction for me, one thing to the pupil next to me who had a different physical structure, another correction to the next, and so on. In short, he possessed a perfectly balanced individual approach, which is the most difficult thing to be developed in a teacher of the dance.

A particularity was his selection in working the muscles of the body successively. As a perfect draughtsman, knowing precisely the anatomy of the human body, his method alternatively gave work and rest to various sets of muscles. His scientific formula was to execute a rhythm of relax and stretch. His was a knowledge of how to work without strain; how to get the most benefit from the physical effort. By this method he sculptured the whole body harmoniously and rhythmically.

Unfortunately at present these precepts are forgotten. Consequently we have increased cramps, adhesions and injuries. Today dancers suffer from numerous twists and strains, torn ligaments and cartilages. In Legat's class such things never happened.

Legat's teaching was wise, if one may so express it. How perfectly he understood the decisive role of bodily proportion in the art of dance, and by his skill prepared each pupil for his creative future.[4]

From 1905 to 1914, Legat enjoyed an unparalleled position as first dancer and ballet master at the Maryinsky, but choreographically he never excelled after losing the collaboration of his brother. When he danced some of Serge's roles he was adversely criticised. Nicolas was proud and arrogant and did not take kindly to criticism from the layman "who did not understand that ease and lightness comes from the height of artistry."

One of Legat's finest roles was the poet Gringoire in *Esmeralda*. When he first performed the role in 1904, he achieved no particular success. Three years later, when he next appeared in the part, he had developed his interpretation and astounded the public with his revised performance.

Ten years after the première, *Esmeralda* was given at a gala performance to mark the twenty-fifth anniversary of Legat's work with the Imperial Theatres. It was a very moving occasion at which Legat gave an unforgettable rendering of Gringoire. It is said that the ovation accorded him lasted fifteen minutes. At the conclusion tables were brought on stage loaded with gifts.

Theatre Review, St. Petersburg, February 11, 1914, described the occasion:

The Benefit Performance was attended by the Emperor Nicolas II and the Empress Maria Feodorovna, together with the Princesses Olga, Maria, and Anastasia, and members of the Imperial Family. When the curtain rose at the end of the performance the hero of the day appeared surrounded by the whole troupe. The first person to greet Legat was Paul Gerdt, who presented him with a garland on behalf of his comrades-actors: "To a beloved friend with gratitude for the preservation of the pure art." The second tribute was from the Imperial Moscow Ballet led by two ballerinas, Morolova and Makletskaya. Then Mr. Bolshakov presented a garland from the Imperial Russian Opera and spoke some words. Mr. Korvin-Kruckovsky made a speech on behalf of the Imperial Drama Theatre, followed by Mr. Terrie who spoke for the French Troupe. Mr. Novikov presented a lyre made of flowers from artists of the Dance School. A student shouted some words from the gallery. To conclude the celebration many greetings and telegrams from ballet dancers were read. There was much applause, and the curtain went up three times.

At the conclusion, Legat made the following speech:

Don't be born good-looking, be born happy. [Words of an old Russian proverb.] For my benefit performance I thought at first to stage *The White Lily* by Asafiev, but illness spoiled my plans for this season. For twenty-five years I have worked and almost never been ill, and then, when I have a benefit performance, I had to take to my bed. What the future holds for me after this performance, unfortunately, I do not know. . . . I am very glad that I was able to work during such a great period, and

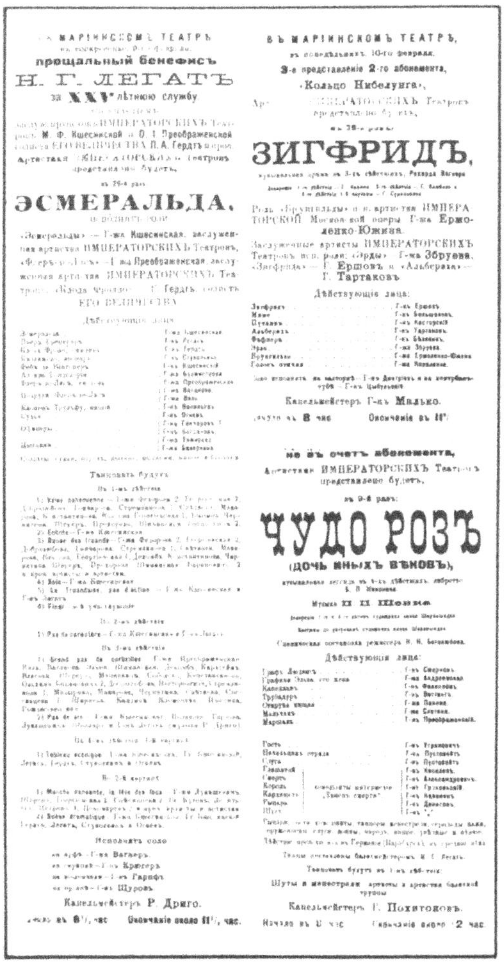

прощальный бенефисъ
Н. Г. ЛЕГАТЪ
за XXV-лѣтнюю службу
ЭСМЕРАЛЬДА.
ВЪ МАРІИНСКОМЪ ТЕАТРѢ,
3-е представленіе 2-го абонемента,
«Кольцо Нибелунга»,
ЗИГФРИДЪ,
Дѣйствующія лица:
Капельмейстеръ Г-нъ Малько.
не въ счетъ абонемента,
ЧУДО РОЗЪ
(ДОЧЬ ИНЫХЪ ВѢКОВЪ),
Дѣйствующія лица:
Капельмейстеръ Р. Дриго.

Detail from the program of the benefit performance of Nicolas Legat, 9 February 1914.

Anna Pavlova and Nicolas Legat in Swan Lake.

that I could remain faithful to the traditions of the classic ballet. I am not inclined to new trends, and for this reason I am considered to be backward. If I do not stay on the Imperial stage, I shall tour abroad. I have received many invitations to teach, but for the present I have declined them.

Legat married first Antonia Chumakova, a dancer, at the Russian church in Paris in 1909. She bore him a daughter Maria, on April 4th of the following year, who died in the siege of Leningrad. Her granddaughter, Tatiana Legat, survived and is a dancer and teacher with the Kirov Ballet. Her husband was the late Yuri Soloviev, one of the Kirov's most brilliant stars. Their daughter, Alena, great-granddaughter of Nicolas, is a pupil at the Leningrad Choreographic School today.

Not long after his marriage Legat became

infatuated with a young pupil, Nadine Nicolaeva, who was eventually to become his ballerina, and who was to wield a considerable influence over him. After the benefit performance he obtained extended leave from the Imperial Theatres, and together they toured abroad. They were dancing at the Mogador Theatre in Paris when World War I broke out. With the help of friends in the diplomatic service they were able to make their way to London where Sir Alfred Butt took them under his protection. In the Spring of 1915, they appeared in variety shows at the Coliseum and the Palace Theatre, dancing classical *pas de deux*.

Nadine was not happy in a foreign country during those war-stricken years. The Russian Consul in Hull arranged their passage by fishing boat to Stockholm, and from there they travelled overland, eventually reaching Petrograd in May. It was generally believed that Legat resigned from the Maryinsky because he could not obtain a position there for Nadine Nicolaeva; since she had not been trained in the school, she could not be accepted into the company. For a period they gave performances for troops, and after the Revolution they settled in Moscow.

During this time of great upheaval Legat worked at the Bolshoi Theatre and School, where Nadine Nicolaeva was accepted as a soloist; but there were disagreements and Legat became associated with Akim Volinsky, a critic who had opened his own Academy of Ballet.

By a resolution of the Legal Department of the Second Central District of Moscow, the marriage of Legat and Antonia Chumakova was dissolved on 4 April 1919. The document gave Antonia Legat the right to resume the use of her maiden name and the custody of their daughter.

It is likely that Nicolas and Nadine Nicolaeva were legally married shortly after this. They toured for a while giving performances to Bolshevik soldiers and sailors. Nadine became ill

Legat in some of his roles at the Maryinsky (left to right): Caprice of the Butterfly, Petrouchka, *Mars in* Blue Beard, Fairy Doll.

in the town of Kharkov, and they decided to settle there, opening a school which soon had over a hundred pupils. Eventually they were ordered to return to Moscow and during the next two years they were involved in intrigues with the Commissars of Culture and the management of the Academic Theatres. A letter of criticism was sent to Lunacharsky, the first Commissar of the Arts, and an article under Legat's name appeared in one of the leading art journals severely criticising the direction of the Academic Theatre School. Inevitably in such tumultuous times artistic standards had fallen. Legat's supporters wanted him to take over the direction of the school and company, a position for which he was not equipped. Nicolas appears to have been a victim, rather than an aggressor, in the jockeying for artistic leadership.

As it turned out, one of his pupils, a brilliant technician, Agrippina Vaganova, was destined to take the highest office and direct the future course of Soviet ballet. For a time, Legat continued to dance and teach independently, but the situation was becoming untenable. Living conditions were gruesome; the future for all artists was perilous. Frustrated and out of favor Nadine became ill again. She developed consumptive glands in her neck, and was sent to a sanatorium in the Crimea. Here her condition worsened, and they despaired of her life. However, a medical board was arranged for her in Moscow, and leave abroad for six months was granted; Nicolas, as husband, was permitted to accompany her.

The Legats left Russia in 1922. They went first to Berlin and Paris, where in his prime Nicolas had enjoyed triumphal seasons with Pavlova and Kschesinska, and then settled in London to dance in the music halls and to teach. In 1925, he accepted the position of ballet master with Diaghilev's Ballet Russe and taught the company in Paris and Monte Carlo. The association was short-lived. Madame Legat, who was engaged as a soloist with the company, was unhappy with her roles, and

the maestro was unhappy with the standard of the dancers, who had been recruited from many sources and danced with the characteristics of different schools. The disenchantment led to rows. Legat resigned and for a time taught in Paris at Salle Wacker. A little later Madame Legat followed him. Presently he returned to London to spend the last twelve years of his life teaching in Colet Gardens, where he gave classes to the young dancers who were to lay the foundations of British ballet.

At various times he made attempts to create his own company without success. During the early thirties he became associated with the Camargo Society, which was trying to establish the roots of a national company in London, and for it he made three ballets. But they were not successful.

During these years his relationship with his wife was less than harmonious. Her restless, dominant nature led her to pursue other avenues. She took two male partners, Sir Paul Dukes and Serge Renoff, with whom she danced in music halls and revues. These engagements took her away for months at a time, until she eventually sustained an injury to her knee which brought an end to her stage career.

An early picture of Nicolas Legat and his partner Nadine Nicolaeva.

In London ballet was at last beginning to take hold; the period of gestation was over. Younger protagonists were entering the field. Legat's studio was a center of germination where dancers came from many countries to learn his extraordinary artistry and magic. From his lustre and his knowledge they received inspiration to go forward in their art and to create in their own way.

Undoubtedly in his last years Legat was a sad and lonely man, weakened by illness and out of touch with a changing world. But, to the last, his skill as a teacher was unimpaired; his gift as a caricaturist and his unquenchable sense of humour never left him. Even when he was dying he sat up in bed drawing innumerable faces. He passed away on 24 January 1937.

---

1. *Story of the Russian School,* Nicolas Legat, London 1932.
2. *The Russian Ballet Theatre of the 20th Century,* Vera Krasovskaya, Leningrad 1958.
3. *Forty Years In Ballet,* Fedor Lopukov, Moscow 1966.
4. *Ibid.*

A Sentimental Poem

Photograph of Legat in London. This picture was sent by him to his daughter in Leningrad and is inscribed: "To my dear daughter Murotchka from your loving, your unhappy father. London, 8 May 1931."

I think of Russia and I cry,
  How long since I have seen
  Your towns and villages
Your trees and fields of green?

There I was happy,
  Loving and beloved;
But long years have I travelled
Through the world,
  And travelling proved
That Russia was my Queen!

Nicolas Legat

Legat's Genius: Tributes from Leading Dancers and Pupils

NOT EVERY DANCER who entered the immense and magnificent studio of Nicolas Legat in Colet Gardens could appreciate the wealth of knowledge and skill that was to be acquired there. Many students could not understand his broken gibberish or his quips in Russian, and many were baffled by his unusual rhythms and the flood of invention. They could not begin to appreciate his refinements of style and his exquisite movement. Some could not get past the barrier of the formidable maestro and found his class incomprehensible. It was necessary to reach the inner man; you had to be humble; you had to be willing to renounce what you had learned before and start afresh.

Anna Roje, who became one of his favorite pupils, tells how, upon arrival at his studio as an established ballerina from Zagreb, she was not permitted to dance in his class. He would not allow her to execute a single *enchaînement,* but insisted upon her doing only *barre*-work for six months, until her faults and placing were remedied. He insisted upon correct beginnings.

I have only heard one fine dancer speak less than enthusiastically of Legat: Phyllis Bedells. She told me how his class was sometimes cluttered with non-dancers whom he praised excessively, much to her disgust. "How can you say it is good, maestro," she once chided him, "when they are so bad?" To which he replied with a bland smile, "They are enjoying themselves. Why disillusion them? They will never dance anyway."

There is doubtless more than a grain of truth in her statement. Legat praised, as all Russians do, and who would deny that praise sweetens all things? The old man could lavish his Russian charm with a penetrating glow sufficient to melt an ice-cap, and at the same time release barbs of wit that would cut through steel. "Harasho! Magnifique!" he would say to a particularly clumsy woman, and with a disarming smile that disguised any sign of malice, his aside in his own tongue would be, "Dog up a lamp-post!"

One of the most impressive and convincing tributes to Legat's greatness comes from the pen of Fedor Vassilevitch Lopukov, a leading ballet master in the Soviet. In his book *Forty Years in Ballet,* he writes:

> It is sad that these days the name of Legat is rarely remembered. The omission is probably due in part to his departure abroad in 1922, leaving his country forever, and thus separating his personal fate from the fate of the Russian ballet. In spite of this, it is good to remember him, because he was among the finest of teachers who laid the foundations of the present Russian ballet.
>
> How often dancers are not chosen for the perfection of their physical bodies. . . . A good teacher must possess a sharp eye in the selection of dancers so that he may help them to develop their physical bodies and souls in the right direction. N.G. Legat, my teacher and the teacher of A. Vaganova, who owes him so much, although she speaks so obscurely about it, was such a teacher.
>
> Legat did not simply pass on to his pupils that

which he had received from his teachers. He constantly and insistently worked to evolve and perfect a unique system from the genuine national elements of the classical dance. His students did not belong to the French school (as some balletomanes believed); they were the brilliant representatives of a new school of dance—a true Russian classical dance which has indeed conquered the whole world.

More than fifty years have passed since the time I stopped taking classes with Legat. Many of my teachers and colleagues I have forgotten, but the memory of Legat and his classes, I preserve with gratitude.

The following are further tributes to Legat:

Sir Frederick Ashton:

I didn't work long with him but, when I did, I found his classes very inspiring and enjoyable, and I was always fascinated by his charming personality and humor.

He was undoubtedly a great teacher but I was too inexperienced at the time to get the full benefit of his great knowledge.

Alan Carter:

History is, I suppose, a maze of far-fetched coincidences. Certainly my introduction to Monsieur Legat was full of unlikelies.

At the age of nine I was sent to have some classes with the local R.A.D. teacher in Tunbridge Wells, where we lived. She laboriously taught me the first five "Operatic Dancing" grades, in company with two "serious" girl students. Reasonably, my doctor had suggested this treatment to build up my slight physique. Unreasonably, I liked it! It was not proper for little boys to like dancing in those days. I rushed through the childrens' dancing examinations with honors, plus excessive encouragement from the examiners. Of course I was one in a million, being the only male candidate to date.

On reaching the sophisticated age of ten and a half, I was examined by my assembled family, mother, father and two aunts—I am an only child. Questions were put to me, serious and irrevocable. My school report was not brilliant, but my dancing had made unusual progress. Did I want to dance? Of course! Seriously? Of course! In that case it should be really serious, no nonsense.

My aunt was able to arrange a meeting with Leonide Massine who was directing the dances for Cochran's musical *Helen* at the London Pavilion. At a dress rehearsal my aunt and I sat in the stalls and watched George Robey, unable to speak his oracular lines from an altar belching with stage-smoke. Massine came to us at the back of the stalls. He looked me in the eye and told me to accompany him to "meet ze greatest teacher of ze classique ballet."

An hour later I found myself in a vast ballet studio in Colet Gardens, Baron's Court. Massine was in dapper practice costume, Spanish trousers, not tights. He never wore tights because of his bandy legs and lack of instep. I had a comic green tunic down to the top of my

Caricature of Nadine Nicolaeva-Legat.

Seraphina Astafieva brings the vanguard of Russian ballet school to Chelsea, London

thighs, bare swing-back legs, very knobby knees and flattish feet.

Monsieur Legat greeted Massine with a firm handshake and a kiss on both cheeks. Neither were tall men, but Legat had the Yul Brynner "hair-cut" whereas Massine was dark-haired. Legat shook my hand and surveyed me with mock ferocity. He waved us both towards the *barre,* and then sat at the piano and played some introductory chords. I stood behind Massine.

We were guided through the *barre*-work by the master's instructions and the marvelously extemporised music on the piano. Legat spoke in Russian all the time except for the French terminology used for the exercises. Naturally my French names of the steps had an R.A.D.-Tunbridge Wells-Kent accent, whereas Legat gave the same words a Russian twist and thrust. Verbally I understood nothing, but visually I watched Massine, and was able to follow very well. In fact so well, that my *barre*-work had a slight edge over Massine's, and evoked a "good boy" from the master.

In the center, away from the steadying influence of the *barre*, the story was quite different. To my amazement, the master demonstrated the steps and combinations using only his meticulous hands: beating hands; brushing hands; sharp, soft, vibrating hands. They were surprising hands. His body would accompany his hands to indicate subtle technical inflections. Massine's immediate grasp of fantastically complicated *enchaînements* and technical feats of great brilliance left me literally standing; in fact shaking with wonder and excitement. All too soon the lesson was over and the greetings of meeting were repeated. Massine did not speak again, nor did the master. For myself, I was too overwhelmed to breathe.

The family decided that Legat was too advanced for me at that stage, so I was introduced to Princess Seraphina Astafieva, Markova's and Dolin's teacher, and the Lilac Fairy for Diaghilev.

Astafieva was tall, exotic—probably erotic—a madly theatrical character, teaching with passion and endurance in her King's Road, Chelsea, studio: the Pheasantry. Being shy and retiring for the most part, I was terrified when, after class one day, she stood ready to cross the road from the Pheasantry to her "leetle resturrang" opposite, and demanded my arm to lean upon. She was twice my height at the time. All the King's Roaders stopped to watch this great lady *bourrée*-ing across the busy street in high-heeled pale blue bedroom slippers, garnished with ostrich feathers; a turban graced with a vast oriental jewel; pink tights and practice skirt, strung up like a fully-rigged four-master, much higher than normal decency required. She used her long ebony walking stick to stop traffic, smiling regally at the sharply braking vehicles, and emitting disciplined smoke-rings from her black Russian cigarette balanced precariously at the end of a long cigarette holder, her eyes twinkling merrily through mascara and brown eye make-up. Chelsea has tried ever since to regain this summit of panache, elegance and nonconformity.

Each week I left my lessons at home and serious practice in my little studio to travel from Tunbridge to London to study with the Princess. I shared private lessons with Peggy Hookham (Margot Fonteyn) who had just returned from China with her mum. My mum and her mum used to sit on the coal-box lid in the Chelsea studio and watch their offsprings attempting to follow the enthusiastic and expert instructions. The Princess would bash her long stick and count sonorously, "E-vun, e-too, e-tree, e-fvar, darlink!" Or, in a temper, she would turn *pirouettes* and brandish her stick at us all, particularly at the pianist. The latter, Ronnie [Mrs. Veronica Moore Longville], sat at a large grand piano covered with a tiger-skin; she wore large glasses that magnified her eyes, making her look like another tiger. Astafieva often became intolerant with Ronnie's music, but Ronnie did not betray her chagrin at all. Only much later, when I was almost fourteen, did Ronnie disclose her very sympathetic and generous nature.

It was at the last private lesson the Princess ever gave. She suddenly decided she was definitely dying, and that she would teach me one of Nijinsky's *enchaînements* from *Le Spectre de la Rose*. As the Princess staggered through the dance Ronnie began to cry, and so did I. We knew she had been ailing but her spirit was so alive and vibrant that her death seemed impossible. Alas, I never saw her again. She died during the summer: the Lilac Fairy left us in the summer.

Now the time had come to go back to Legat. I was now able to understand and attempt most of the basic classical steps. I had also studied, during my one day in town per week, acting, singing and other kinds of dancing, as well as the Cecchetti dance method.

The Baron's Court studio still seemed enormous; but the master, rhythmically, imperturbably watering the floor (to give it the right surface for dancing), appeared smaller after the Princess's towering height. The atmosphere in this very high-pitched studio (it had been built for a monumental sculptor) was mysterious, and I immediately felt like a royal duke in a vast palace ballroom. Round the walls were a number of very funny colored caricatures of ballet dancers and personalities. The master was prodigiously adept at evoking likenesses of faces and bodies and the studio was much enlivened by this graphic humor. He was also a considerable musician, playing the piano extempore for all his classes, and twanging a merry balalaika on Sundays in concert with an orchestra of emigré White Russians. Sometimes the studio resembled an exotic musical instrument museum with balalaikas of all shapes and sizes draped around the walls.

To my lasting sorrow I did not learn Russian, and my dear master did not learn English, ex-

Agrippina Vaganova.

cept for a few pidgin phrases, graphically expressive, but not always explicit in their meaning. Contrary to present practice, he allowed visitors to watch the classes. We sometimes had a bevy of distinguished impresarios, ex-dancers, theatrical agents, fans and mothers watching from a row of tip-up theatre seats installed for that purpose. Legat would sometimes turn to one of these onlookers sitting nearest to the piano, and whisper loudly what he thought of a particular pupil. Once he said to a doting mother, "She verra goot dancer but . . . not today . . . not tomorrow . . . not in hundred years!" Neither mother nor daughter returned again to sample the master's wit or knowledge.

Undoubtedly a considerable number of students did not return after one or two classes. Legat seldom made any comment or correction until the pupil had had a chance to assimilate the structure of his lessons, and this might take up to a year. Indeed many of us were so confused and deflated by our obvious non-comprehension of the master's simplest directions that we had to steel ourselves in order to continue. But Legat noticed our discomfort and encouraged us with, "Leetel by leetel." I, at least, was totally won over by his patient quietness. Sometimes one of the pupils would be on form in *pirouettes*, and shower the audience with beads of sweat. Legat would recommend an umbrella. Or ill-fixed hair-dos would disintegrate in lethal volleys of hairpins peppering the spectators. Legat would lift the lid of the piano and hide his head while continuing to play with the other hand. Occasionally he would rise from the piano with stately purpose and cross the studio with deliberate step to demonstrate or give a judicious prod in the appropriate hip or back or head or muscle of an offending dancer. On the way back to the piano he would invariably crack a joke in Russian which made those who could understand double up with hysterics. Gradually I began to get the gist of his jokes, but too vaguely alas to recount.

His English never advanced beyond basic pidgin. He used a few picturesque words to formulate his conversations. These took me months to understand, but finally made sense. Such expressions as "ture-darn; lyka sorsaage; stronk-bak; worr tis dis; gut-boie; you no spik my vife, she no understan." These injunctions, coupled with onomatopoetic additions, were used more or less to cover all exigencies. Crazily enough they did. Being able to accompany his own lessons on the piano, he was able to guide the pupil by the rhythms of the steps, a facility he acquired over years as a first-class ballet-master of stars of the first rank.

Legat taught a subtle *épaulement*, which gave lightness and quickness even to gargantuan dancers. He explained how an almost imperceptible change in the angle of the hips could effect *pirouettes* and balance. He taught where to focus the eyes when turning; how to correct or give special accent on turning steps; how to add *battu* to almost every known step; how the arms must always be perfect in shape from any angle; how and where to accent standard combinations; and how the body's weight can be used like a pendulum. Whatever he taught, it was always infused with the idea of classicism, of perfection, and not of trickery or strain or gimmickry. That was what impressed me then, and impresses me even more now. Indeed I find myself rethinking steps and combinations of steps in his way, as if he were still guiding me. He also taught me the importance of shape and form: a chair balances because it remains in its shape, whereas a piece of string falls limp; or facial strain betrays incorrect use of the neck and diaphragm muscles.

He taught me the double *tour en l'air* which had evaded me for some time. Suddenly one day I could do it—and not only to one side. Because of his insistence on training equally both right and left, I was able to *pirouette* or turn or jump equally in both directions. In spite of the very considerable technical improvement generally amongst dancers, I am still horrified by the absurd pedagogic attitude of even very famous teachers of ballet who perpetrate, "Do it the best side dear. No point in doing it the hard way." This is like advocating swimming with the right leg and arm only. Of course everyone tends to be one-sided, but then education of any kind is supposed to teach one what one can't do, or doesn't know. Anyway, for myself, after training with Legat, I did not have to distinguish between right and left, for they were trained equally.

I have always followed Legat's teaching, although I do not copy him. That is what he taught: to rethink, understand and develop, but not to copy. Each body has its own beauty which must learn to conform to the technique in its own way. Technique itself is a living, growing thing, and must adapt and encompass new things. A master is greater than a method, because the master can adjust and change to suit the contingency. A master must visualise perfection and transmit it to his pupils; this is classicism. If I am nonplussed by a technical point, I try to rethink it through his eyes. Legat's way was the classical way. It takes longer and requires great care and thought, but it provides a better and finer solution than any glossing over method or rule of thumb. Pupils must be guided and not bullied; they must learn to contribute with mind and body, and not be desiccated sausages. Frigidity is anathema to art. The body and the mind must be flexed and flexible.

All the leading Russian dancers had worked with Legat at one time or another in Russia, and all the emigrés visited him and revered him, at first in Paris and then in London.

On one occasion the huge studio was further enlarged and a stage built at one end for a performance. An astonishing number of famous dancers appeared to honor the master. Even his wife returned and interfered, between practicing *développés* with weights attached to her legs. The music was beautifully chosen and played on two pianos, Vladimir Launitz sharing the accompanying with the master. In retrospect one number still amazes me. It was for six girls, I think, all famous dancers—and now teachers. The choreography was abstract and would even appear to be modern today, I believe; certainly post-Fokine.

But now the dear old man was beginning to

Some of the last drawings made by Legat lying in his sick bed.

decline. He felt the cold. The one anthracite stove heated a few feet of one end of the vast room, while Legat froze at the other. His wife sometimes popped in and out and seemed to irritate him, although he was always well-mannered and good tempered. There were days when he could not give the Class of Perfection, and his wife took over. It was not the same. She was energetic and by no means without ability and knowledge, but her mind was not classic. Truly she taught some of the master's tricks of the trade, but, as I thought, in exaggerated forms, and usually to students long before they were ready for such advanced work.

Time was running on. I was almost sixteen; time to look for a job. Ninette de Valois auditioned me for the Wells, the Vic-Wells Ballet. She laughed with Irish frenzy when she saw my *grand battement*—above hip-level—something unknown among English male dancers of that era. Later she exploded into fits of spastic-like choreography when she "experienced" my *pirouettes*! They were numerous, multiple and equal to the right and left. She was by no means a fan of Legat's, although she admitted that he was a great teacher. Her irascible, forceful nature could not allow the old man's masculine approach. I suspect, too, that his wife had offered terrible and unforgettable insults to "the Irish woman with the French Royal Family name, and her terrible English amateurs." This was a great pity. Legat could have given the English Company a great deal in the early days, not least the nobility of style and attack which has since taken so long to acquire. It is an example of her greatness, I think, that Ninette did engage me on the spot, and offered me thirty shillings per week, in spite of her disapproval of the master.

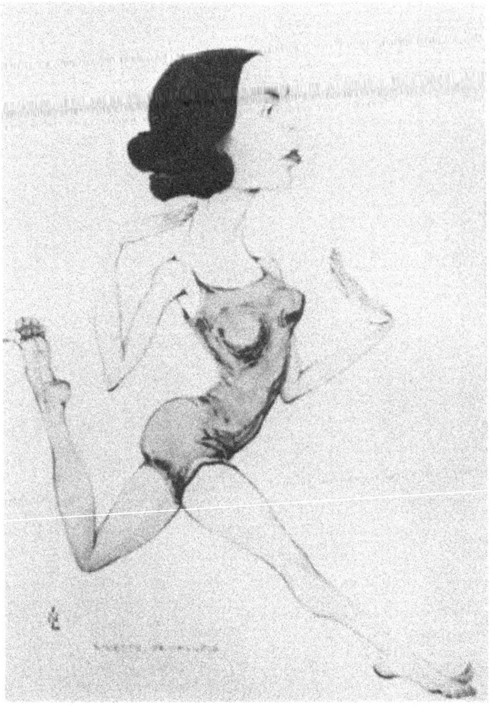

Ninette de Valois.

Legat was upset, but understanding. He was often bed-ridden and seldom able to take even his Class of Perfection. I returned whenever possible to take classes and to see him. He recovered sufficiently at one point to visit my family's house. He played on my piano and insisted that I play to him afterwards. Then we improvised a duet: "Vera gut; not lika sorsaage!"

A little later Madame Legat gave an enormous party in the big studio, but the old man couldn't make it. I went to see him in his bed. He was uncharacteristically unshaven, both face and pate. He tried to talk to me, but was soon defeated by the deafening row from the party above that made the rafters shake with merriment. He spoke in Russian; Anna Roje translated. I was lost in a sea of tears and unspoken thought. There was nothing I could do but rush out of his room and get the Baron's Court tube to go home. Even on the underground I could still hear the gaiety of the party.

Nadine Nicolaeva-Legat.

A short time later he died. André Eglevsky stood vigil all night over the coffin in the great studio. An enormous painting of Pavlova, one of his favorites, leaned outwards precariously from its hook on the wall, as if flying over his body like a guardian angel. Then came the Russian church service. We all stood; no chairs or pews. The great bass voice of the priest and the incredibly sonorous choir penetrated the gloom. A lot of people, many weeping, including the widow, were there. In my youthful sincerity I felt surrounded by crocodiles. So many of those people had said such bad things about the old man. Now they filed round the church, queueing up to kiss his body. I held my mother's hand tight and tried not to cry. Tears, I felt, were shed by his enemies. Humor and the perpetuation of his teaching would be more useful and more sincere to his memory.

The famous caricatures on the walls of the studio seemed more poignant and precious; a wisp of hilarity in death—Til Eulenspiegelish! Unquestionably he is still part of me.

Anton Dolin.

Anton Dolin:

I can say with truth that, not only did I know Nicolas Legat, but that a mutual and sincere affection existed between master and pupil.

Not many years after the First World War, Legat and his wife, Nadine Nicolaeva, arrived in London, and for several wonderful months I had the great good fortune to study with him. In those early days there were not many pupils to whom he imparted his unparalleled knowledge of the true art of ballet, but the quiet almost religious way he taught us by his own Legat method was a revelation.

A small drill-hall near Swiss Cottage served as his studio. The floor was by no means good for dancing, but in those days dancers were not as spoilt (happily perhaps) as they are today. Legat rarely got up from the piano as he taught; he sat there playing the charming little tunes which he had composed for the exercises. Only when we stupidly (which in my case was often) could not grasp his *enchaînements,* would he rise from the piano and come over quietly to show what he wanted.

It was in his studio that I had my first electrifying encounter with the great Anna Pavlova, when she came one day to visit him. Of course I showed off before her even more than usual. She spoke to me. "One day you will be a fine dancer, you will join my company, and, who knows, even dance with me." Alas, I never did, for some time later I became a member of Serge Diaghilev's Ballet Russe. Still, the encouraging words of the great ballerina were an incentive to work even harder than before, and whatever fame I may have achieved in later years, believe me, did not come without blood, sweat and tears.

Dear Kolya Legat. He was indeed a great teacher. He taught me so much, including the art of *pas de deux,* for which I am so grateful. He also paid me the compliment of calling me "Piccadilly." He left behind a system of teaching, a literature of dance, which, as I have said, is the true art of ballet.

Barbara Gregory:

The overwhelming impression that the Legat studio first made upon me was that here dancing was an expression; mechanics did not intrude. Every movement flowed with an animation that I had not believed possible in my dance training. The *pas de basque* was like a joyous bubble of mirth, not the set one, two, three that I had known. The *attitude* inclined to the audience, giving out an abundance. I had known it as an upright position, angular and straight. *Pirouettes* were light and quick and simply unfolded out of a variety of *allegro* steps. No visible preparation. They expressed excitement, happiness.

I was in tears after my first class with Nicolas Legat. But from then on I could never look back. I became dedicated to his joyous way of dancing, and never in all my travels have I found a system to equal it in beauty or technical skill. His remains a master class.

In the Colet Gardens studio there was a joy in learning to dance; no drudgery, no fear. "Leetle by leetle" was one of the few English expressions Legat acquired. If one fell off a *pirouette* it was no sin, but a chance for mirth, which Legat expressed by running his thumb nail down the piano keys. His studio was large, and a series of simple *glissades jetés en diagonale* became like a flight of birds simply because the *jeté* commenced from a little *arabesque,* not from a brush in front of the body, as I had known it. *Piqué manège* became a relay race, as he called, "caf to caf," meaning don't lift the back leg, but fit the calf muscle to the calf muscle. Oh, the speed it gave! And so, gradually I understood his secrets, learning by watching both the good and the bad dancers, for one's eyes soon learned to select, and see what not to do.

In the Legat class there were decisive differences in the execution of certain steps and positions for male dancers. For instance, boys were not permitted to do *pas de chat,* which he considered a girl's step. They performed a *brisé* instead of a *pas de chat. Arabesques* were never lifted above waist level. The *pirouette* was performed with the working foot *sur le cou-de-pied,* no higher. Boys never picked up their feet in a *pas de bourrée* (*pizzicato* fashion); they performed only simple *pas de bourrée* close to the floor. If an *attitude* was given looking under the arm, the boy held a more upright pose than the girl, with less head inclination. All these are small details which added more masculinity and style to the male dancer.

The wonderful use of *épaulement* was a new discovery in the language of dance—so simple, yet so seldom correctly understood. When the body turns *en diagonale* the head remains to the front, the eyes looking out, direct, at eye-level. The slight inclination incurred causes the head to fall into line with the body, elongating the whole form, and thus presenting the longest and most elegant line. And not only does it give line, but perfection of balance and technique—the weight of the body being constantly transferred to the supporting leg.

With the mastery of *épaulement* come the flowing arm movements, the ever curved elbow in *arabesque* (I had known it as a straight line) giving the additional possibility that the movement was never finished, but could move on to further extension. The balance of the body is at all times slightly forward. Nicolaeva, his wife, once pointed out to me that no good sculpture stands solidly on its base, but has an inclination forward—the difference between dead and living sculpture.

How elegant and stylish those dancers who knew and understood these rules looked in his class, always standing in the *croisé* position to commence an *enchaînement.* "Only an amateur would stand in *effacé,*" were Legat's words told me by his wife. After his death, when I continued to study with Madame Legat, she discussed his theories with me, and it is perhaps to her I owe a debt for the clarity she brought to these explanations. She was an enigma of a woman, so utterly the opposite of her husband in temperament and in her attitude towards teaching. Legat was tranquil, persuasive, never forcing, whereas she was dynamic, forceful and dominating. To my mind she had an incredible knowledge of dance technique, but it must be admitted that she lacked discretion and diplomacy. However, it must also be granted that, as she herself said, she could teach a cow to dance!

From her I learned the reasoning behind the structure of the class. Everything was balanced, never too much of one movement in one direction; an exercise of tension being counter-balanced by one of relaxation; a step of rebounding *allegro* followed by one of *legato;* the small *allegro* leading to the big *allegro,* and so on to the *batterie* and *grands tours.* The *enchaînements* were endless in variation and rhythm. How mentally alert one had to be to catch them quickly, but how exhilarating and exciting each new possibility.

After many years of teaching it is still exciting to teach this method, to discover in every class a new possibility of combinations like the never-ending combinations of notes and harmonies in musical scoring. I am ever grateful for the joy in dance that Nicolas Legat imparted.

Patrick Hall:

Long before I was a dancer with Sadler's Wells Ballet, and later a stage director at the Royal Opera House, I was an habitué of Colet Gardens, and remember one or two amusing incidents. The first concerns Legat's very odd, and at times incomprehensible English.

One day finding himself in the back streets of Soho, the maestro inquired of a policeman the way to Leicester Square. When the officer had explained the direction Legat, with all his charming courtesy, made a bold effort to thank him. Clicking his heels and bowing graciously, he uttered the following sentence, which he had probably confused with words he had learned to welcome visitors to the studio: "Thank you very much, too much, sit down, please!" One can imagine the bewildered policeman's reaction.

In the class his excursions into English were at times hilarious, and his corrections were delivered with a great deal of humor. For instance, "head up" was "keep your football up," "body upright" was "keep very Oxford

Legat on the balcony of his Colet Court studio. Taken by Zelia Raye during the last year of his life.

Street," and "relax" was "now you can Leicester Square."

Behind glass doors at the entrance to the studio stood a bronze bust of Legat. A favorite trick of his was to stand in front of the glass doors, exactly opposite the bust, and pretend that it was his reflection. When he had gained complete stillness, so that it was impossible to tell whether it was the bust or the reflection, Legat would suddenly grimace like a monkey, making the statue come to life, much to the merriment and laughter of his pupils. He was always given to such antics, and was perfectly enchanting with children.

On another occasion, there was a crisis at the studio when funds were short, and there was insufficient money to pay the monthly rent. It was before the advent of Captain Tchapline, who later became his efficient secretary and kept such matters in order. After hurried consultations with friends and associates, it was advised that the master himself should approach Lady Moyne, mother of Grania Guiness (at the time a young pupil), and put out feelers for a loan. Legat understood well that to ask for money directly was a delicate matter, and required discretion and tact. It was utterly distasteful to him, but, having received instruction on how to present his suit without making a bloomer, he approached the lady. Not however, as he had been schooled. When the moment of attack came, his vocabulary

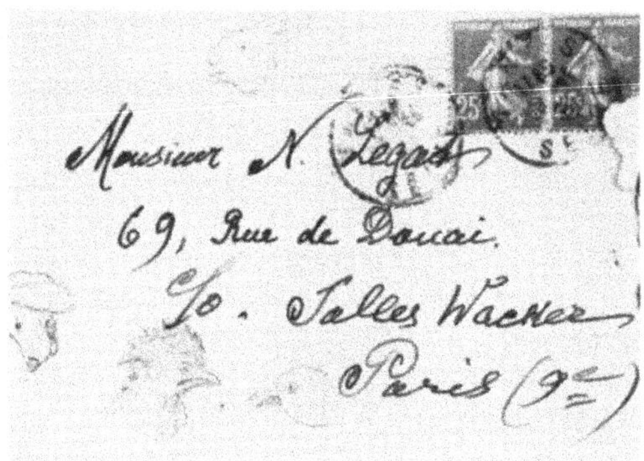

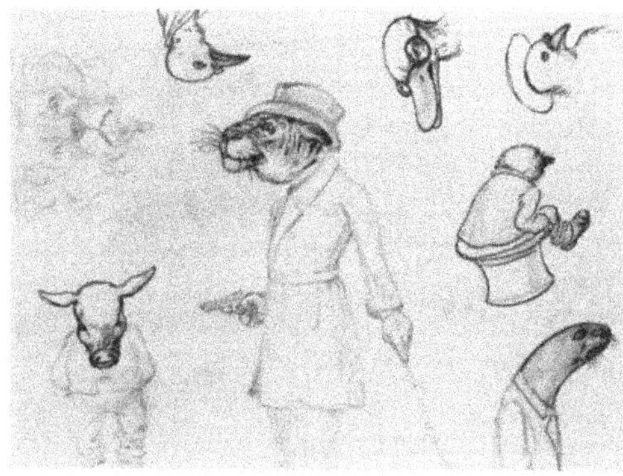

Legat was never idle. Whether he was at home, in the studio, or in a restaurant, he was always busy with pen or pencil, forever doodling. These little animal sketches suggest that he would have made an excellent illustrator of children's books.

failed him utterly; he bowed courteously, and with a disarming smile said bluntly, "Geeve me feefty pounds." His request was instantaneously granted.

More than anything else I recall Legat's phenomenal strength. In the studio, which had a plank floor of pine wood, I remember Legat throwing pennies with such force and precision that they would stick embedded in the floor. Nobody else could accomplish this trick, which required immense skill. This remarkable physical strength stayed with him in his old age, even when he was dying. The doctors, when told of his inexhaustable energies, could not believe he was as ill as he appeared to be. By an effort of the will he would drag himself from a sick bed to give André Eglevsky a class, and when he was restrained from rising and dressing, he would sit up in bed to give Anna Roje, his favorite pupil, a lesson in his bedroom—not the first time he had given class from his bed. With double pneumonia he still could not be confined to his bed, but would force himself to teach. The result of his intrepid will was disastrous; he gradually crumpled as the illness gripped him. His heart gave out, and, suddenly, before anyone could believe it, he was dead. Everybody who frequented the studio was stunned by the loss of this great and lovable man.

Dorothy Lysaght:

Nearly forty years later I can remember the genuine sorrow I shared with the hundreds of pupils and friends who crowded into the Russian Church for his funeral. It is fortunate that people stand for services in the Orthodox churches because we were elbow to elbow from wall to wall; there would have been no room for seats or spaces between them. Every dancer, would-be dancer, dance lover and anyone with a drop of Russian blood was in that church to mourn that terrible loss to the world of dance.

The Marchioness of Normanby Grania Guiness:

My impressions as a child and teenager are distinct. The Legats were in London in 1923. I went for private lessons at the age of three—much too young! Madame taught me and he escaped from the piano occasionally.

Then I believe they must have left England, for I went later to Massine's class (1925 I think), and when he left England, he recommended me to Ninette de Valois, who was running a school in Rowland Gardens with Ursula Moreton. It must have been about two years later, when I was ten, that she went to Sadler's Wells where I had my lessons.

Theodore Kosloff, who had given lessons to

The above drawing is a study Legat made for his famous caricature entitled "The Unholy Trinity." The persons represented are P.J.S. Richardson, founder and editor of the Dancing Times; *Edwin Evans, music and ballet critic of the* Times; *and, below, Arnold Haskell, critic and author of numerous books on ballet, and later head of the Royal Ballet School.*

my mother, insisted that I should go to Legat. I was therefore learning in Colet Gardens, as well as the Cecchetti system at the Wells. Ninette, who was a very sensible person, thought it a good idea and I did not find it too confusing. This must have been in 1932, and Colonel Leontieff (that very nice man) was Mr. Legat's secretary. I had private lessons, and later classes as well.

I think the thing that struck me about Nicolas Legat's teaching, even as a child, was that while he never neglected to correct in detail, one felt that all this was only a means to an end. Of course we all know that this is so theoretically, but with him I was continuously conscious of this striving for perfection. When, for an instant, one was able to show a suggestion of it, he was as thrilled as if one had given him a present.

Ninette was an excellent teacher, as were others I studied under, but I felt from the first day that Legat's lessons were something quite apart from ordinary teaching. He called his class the Class of Perfection, after his class in Russia. It was an apt name.

His stature as a teacher has not been sufficiently recognised.

Dame Alicia Markova:

I went to Mr. Legat as a child and took part in his ballet at the London Palladium. I can remember very little about the choreography; I was too young. Later I received instruction from Mr. Legat when I was with the Diaghilev Ballet. As I remember, Mr. Legat joined in the autumn of 1925, and toured with us to Paris, Switzerland, Italy and Monte Carlo.

He was a very stern teacher, very severe. I think because of this some of the company did not like him. The dancers had been used to the set routines of Cecchetti, whereas Mr. Legat gave different *enchaînements* in every lesson. Legat's method called for close attention and concentration, and this was not popular with everybody. I loved his classes for their lightness and speed. I feel he gave me speed. I was quite terrified of him and one of the funniest

Additional studies for "The Unholy Trinity."

situations, looking back, was taking class with this awesome master in the morning and that same evening dancing Papillon to his Pantaloon in *Carnaval*. I was petrified.

Mr. Legat helped me greatly in 1932, when I was with the Vic-Wells Ballet and about to tackle the full length *Swan Lake*. I needed help with the Ballroom Scene. I took in all, I think, five private lessons with him. He strengthened me and made my *fouettés* secure. For this I have to thank him all my life. His lessons were very expensive, quite beyond my purse at that time, but I used to save in various ways, sometimes by walking to class instead of taking the bus.

I think Mr. Legat left the Diaghilev Ballet for a number of reasons, not just because of a disagreement with Diaghilev. After all, Mr. Legat was getting on in years and travelling was a great strain in those days. He had reached the stage when he wanted to settle down and have his own school, where he could work in his own way without interference.

Leonide Massine:

I knew Nicolas Legat in London, during his Colet Gardens period. I went to him whenever I had the chance. I think I sent Eglevsky to him.

Legat was a logical, precise teacher; his school was scientific, as it should be, not given to fancy just to please the pupils. His school was outstanding. If some people called him the slave of tradition, that is a silly remark. Only an ignorant person could say that. He naturally took the best things from the past; being a musician, an artist, he had all the essentials to be a good professor.

Undoubtedly Legat did not receive the recognition due to him in England. There is a common, banal and commercial attitude in the world of art which is detrimental to all pioneers.

Cleo Nordi:

I hail you dear Nicolas Gustavovitch Legat, artist, genius, inspired teacher of the ballet with its intricate techniques and its fullness of expression.

Over fifty years ago, when I had the privilege to begin my private lessons in the flat on the Petersburg side, Nicolas Legat was using his fiddle for accompaniment, plucking the strings. Unforgettable experience!

I lived every day in great excitement, impatiently waiting for my next lesson, to learn the

Nicolas Legat in Fairy Doll.

mysteries of the true art of classical dance. I felt compelled to record these lessons, and also his wise counsels. Thus, through all my years of study with Monsieur Legat I collected a library of written lessons, which have been a continuous inspiration and divine guidance to me since the time I started to teach.

In Russia, Paris, London, wherever he taught, every dancer great or small, received a new approach to dancing. In many the inherent creative ability was enriched and stimulated. Many dancers became aware of the refinements of *épaulement* and the stylish qualities it imparted to the movement. Legat had a penetrating vision, and brought out in his pupils the ability to dance as human beings, and to realise to the full the expressiveness and plasticity given them by the Divine Creator. His method used every muscle of the body in an harmonious, logical way, in perfect synchronisation. He taught the dancer to execute with ease the technical demands of steps, big and small, in simple and in complicated combinations, embracing the whole range of existing movement.

The essence of the teachings of Nicolas Legat are so profound, so intelligent, so ingenious. To teach his way is nearly impossible. In many parts of the world his pupils are trying to teach his method but unfortunately, in most cases, the method has been misunderstood, and his ideas misrepresented. Before his death, when he was very ill, he honored me by asking me to take care of his morning classes for two weeks. This in some measure confirmed his faith in me as a teacher. I am, I believe, the oldest of his pupils still alive today continuing to teach his method.

Michael Somes, C.B.E.:

His classes were magnificent, human and enjoyable (if impossible!), and one so well remembers having finished the last *pirouette* ages ago, whilst Eglevsky and Alan Carter were still spinning on and on—André ever so slowly—and both until there was no impetus left, and standing on their *demi-pointes* whilst the maestro "glissaded" up and down the keyboard.

I can also remember him showing me the step he said was "the original for Albrecht in the second act of *Giselle,* consisting of three *renversés.*" Needless to say, I never attempted it in public. I'm afraid I was much too "small fry" to dare to do much more than listen, and answer when spoken to; but of course my admiration was immense. He taught me so much, and I thank God for the luck I had to have been in some of his classes.

Jack Spurgeon:

My days with Nicolas Legat are some of the most treasured. Unfortunately, like so many dancers, I had to work and train at the same time, and this I found hard to make Mr. Legat understand. He would say, "You come every day!" I would explain I needed money to live and this often meant going on tour, but he still did not think this necessary and would persist with his, "You come every day!" He little realised how I wished this was possible. In order to attend his master classes it was necessary to cycle (to save money) from north London to Baron's Court, but this I gladly did whenever the opportunity presented itself.

Often after class I would sit and write out the whole lesson, and on one such occasion I was comparing notes with Pearl Argyle when Mr. Legat came by and asked what we were doing. He smiled and shook his head saying, "You should never write down classes; just keep creating them."

Mr. Legat always accompanied his own classes on the piano, which gave added feeling to every *enchaînement* because the music was so appropriate and in such a variety of counts. Often one felt that the music was either swearing at or complimenting the dancers, according to the success they were having with the particular movements involved.

So many great dancers would assemble for class. One admired and marvelled at the way they all became just pupils on an equal footing, such was the discipline that was expected, and willingly given, in the presence of this master of the art of teaching.

Legat showing his grief for the absence of a pupil.

Wendy Toye:

The thing I remember best about studying with Mr. Legat was the extraordinary feeling of lightness that his classes gave me. The studio where he taught at Colet Gardens was very large and extremely high, with many big windows, which was quite unusual in those days. As I remember, most of the studios I had worked in were quite dark, and the electric lights had to be on all the time; here, suddenly, was great space, and airiness and light, brightened even more by this dear good humored man with his devastatingly witty sense of the ridiculous. His vitality and energy seemed to lift one off the floor in an amazing fashion. I swear I was able to jump higher there than anywhere else before or since. He used to take a great delight in making me do the boys' *enchaînements* as well because my elevation was quite good, and he would shout across the huge room, "Vendy vith the boys too, Vendy vith the boys!"

When I first went to study with Mr. Legat I was quite young, twelve or thirteen I should think, and I was in the adult professional class. Naturally, like all newcomers of whatever age, I felt very lost to start with, particularly so because he used to arrange his different *enchaînements* and groups of steps and exercises by using funny little private words and phrases, and never ever saying the actual name of a step. One had been so used to one's teacher saying, "*Pas de basque, temps de flèche,* step, double *pirouette en dedans,*" etc., but the maestro would swivel round on his piano

Grotesque heads drawn by Legat on the backs of cheese boxes.

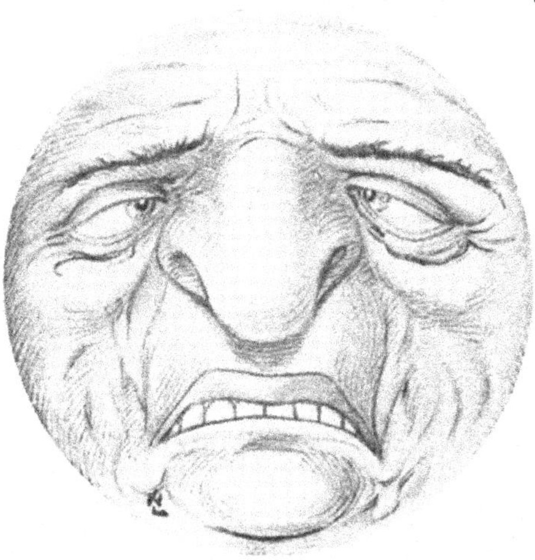

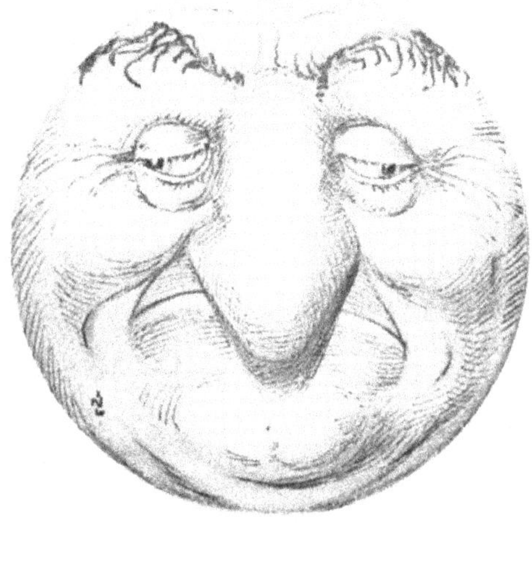

stool, and with his blue eyes twinkling—his very alive hands would twinkle too—indicate how he wanted us to move our feet, while he said things like *"Tsim, tsim, flic flac, poum poum,* tsen repeat laeft fout." Such a beautiful accent it was. His tiny feet would tap out the rhythm; his shoulders would swing in a certain way, and the initiated would know exactly what he meant. But the others hadn't understood a thing! They would flounder at the back, just about having learned the routine from copying the people in front, by the time the maestro was ready to begin the next *enchaînement*: *"Duom, duom, duom, flim flam, flic flac."* Oh, but the joy, when, after a few weeks, he called me to the front of the group to be one of the translators of his personal private language—being there with Eglevsky, and Anna Roje, and sometimes Agnes de Mille, Margot Fonteyn, Patricia Bowman, Pamela May, Harold Turner, June Brae, Alan Carter and others.

He would then turn back to his old upright piano and always play the most enchanting and amusing little tunes, which he would make up on the spot. I never remember him giving the same class twice, which was one of the many joys of learning with him. I often wondered how he could play so continuously and so originally and, at the same time so it seemed, not miss a single fault of anybody's in the whole class. Sitting behind his piano, a continuous stream of bad English and soft flowing Russian issuing forth, from time to time his bald head would bob over the top or round the side of the piano, or he would dart out to adjust a hip, or an *épaulement*, when his English failed him.

The Russian wasn't always complimentary. My sister-in-law, Doris Sonne (one of his favorite pupils), says that when she saw his eyes twinkling brighter and a certain particularly benign expression on his face, she knew he was taking an impish delight in berating his English pupils, who, misled by that guileless smile, thought they were being praised, when, in fact, he was calling them fools with disarming amiability, much to the delight of the Russian-speaking pupils.

Doris once wrote to Mr. Legat to say that she was ill and could not attend classes for a few weeks. Unable to reply in English, the maestro proved himself more eloquent by sending her a delicious caricature of himself crying large tears into a cup. His caricatures are famous, and his brilliance and wittiness in pointing out the weaknesses of the greatest ballerina or cavalier were devastating. One might otherwise never have noticed that particular factor, which again goes to prove his penetrating powers of observation as a critic and as a teacher. All the greats were among his victims, and were very proud to be so, I think.

When Anton Dolin was about fifteen years old and studying with the maestro, he could never understand why Mr. Legat called him "Picci-dilly, Picci-dilly! Do dis Picci-dilly; do dat *flic flac*." How and why this name originated was to remain a mystery until one day two years later when they were on a bus together. Dolin thinks it was a No. 13 from Finchley Road to Oxford Circus, on their way to the London Palladium, where Dolin was dancing with the Moscow Arts Company, partnering Madame Nicolaeva, Legat's wife. When they approached Piccadilly, Legat with great excitement tapped Dolin on the shoulder and pointed towards Piccadilly Circus. "Picci-dilly, Picci-dilly," he said, and then pointed at Dolin again. For a moment the dancer was nonplussed, and the maestro had to repeat himself four or five times before Dolin suddenly realised that Legat was actually pointing at the statue of Eros. Thus did Pat Dolin at last understand the significance of the nickname.

Those were wonderful years when I studied with Mr. Legat. I'm very proud to have been one of his pupils. I remember still his energy, his straight back, his kindness; yet his compellingly strict and brilliant teaching, flavored so richly with his very personal humor. If he arranged an exercise finishing with a *pirouette* and André Eglevsky was in the class, he would accompany us with one of his adorable little tunes, and at the end, while Eglevsky was still continuing his *pirouette* long after we were in the finishing position—fifteen, sixteen, seventeen, on and on—the variations of the turning music would go on and on describing the quality of the *pirouette,* sometimes pretending to stop and then start again, sometimes getting slower and slower, as André's beautifully controlled turns did just that. It was sheer delight! But the maestro *was* sheer delight.

Maria Zybina:

From the moment I joined Mr. Legat's Class of Perfection in London a new life seemed to open before my eyes. I had been trained by several eminent Russian teachers on the continent and enjoyed their classes at which we all worked until we were exhausted. However, this was something different; here with Legat we felt refreshed after finishing a lesson. After some months I still felt the same remarkable effect, so I decided to stay in England and train regularly with Legat. As it happened I was one of the lucky people who lived for a time in the same boarding house as the master.

I found him a most warm-hearted person, but he did not mix easily. Once you knew him and he regarded you as a friend, his personality was exuberant. Then he would open up and expound his inexhaustible knowledge and experience. We often sat up late into the night talking about every kind of dancing, theory, history, and temperaments and habits of different countries and their dance cultures. Mr. Legat was not only a teacher of classical ballet, he also had a wide knowledge of national character and mime. Although he did not give a character class with *barre-* and center-work, as we do today, I am sure that his talks with us had a great influence on my character work. When he choreographed a national dance, his persuasiveness and explanations were all-embracing.

PART II

SEVEN CLASSES BY NICOLAS LEGAT

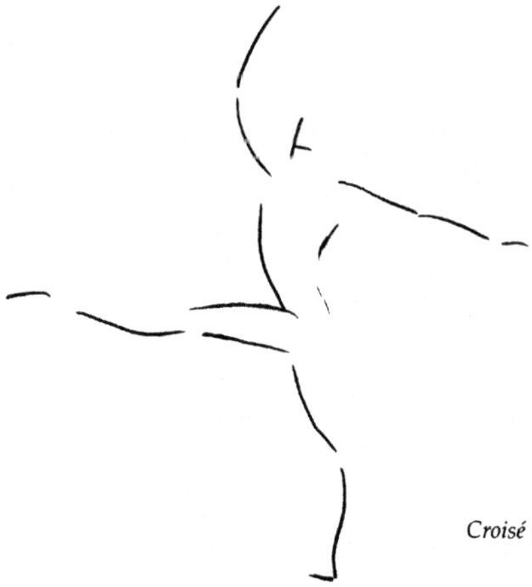

Croisé devant

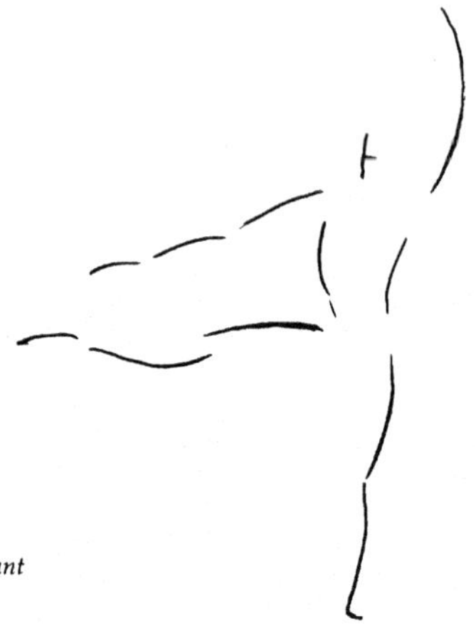

Effacé devant

Attitude effacé

Attitude croisé

Arabesque effacé

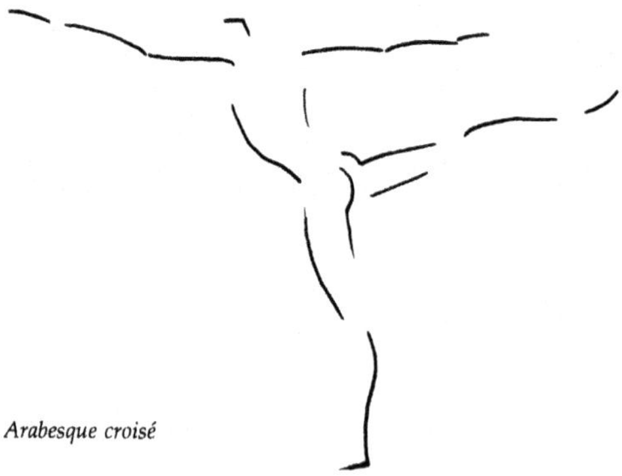

Arabesque croisé

Drawings by Eilean Pearcey.

Introduction to the Classes

THE BASES OF THIS BOOK are the four classes hand-written by Nicolas Legat for André Eglevsky. To broaden the scope of the book, other contributors have been asked to give their versions of Legat classes, and we have placed them so that there is a development and a growing process.

The first class is basic—the kind of simple class a skilled professional dancer needs to keep his trained body in perfect condition while he has to contend with strenuous rehearsals and performances. Other classes are fuller and more complex giving a richness of classical movement.

It is difficult to convey in words the style and quality of a step, but those teachers who have studied Legat and his rhythmic subtleties, *épaulement,* and fluidity and flow, will be able to refresh themselves at the fount. Dancers and teachers with no previous knowledge of the Legat class will surely be able to take some inspiration and enlightenment from this material.

Each class is given, as far as is possible, in the nomenclature of the individual interpreter. However, we have tried to keep uniformity in the presentation of the text. The counts are always given first, on the left, opposite the description of the step, so that the movement may be learned rhythmically from the beginning—rhythm being the key to the correct performance of any *enchaînement.*

The fundamental structure of the class always follows the same form—an ordered logical pattern—but the variations within the framework are infinite. It is this freedom within the whole that enables the system to be creative and progressive, yet remain contemporary.

The order of the exercises has a carefully worked out development designed to bring into play the physical processes of the body with a natural ease and harmony. Every muscle and ligament is exercised systematically, and the circulation of the whole body is generated methodically without any forcing or violent tension. Nurtured in this way the dancer's body becomes a finely tuned instrument with a capacity for physical power and effortless ease.

Aesthetically the line and form of the school is developed with the rules of *épaulement*—the play of the dancer's body from diagonal to diagonal—very rarely using the static *en face* positions. Such rules produce the longest classical lines and most aristocratic style. The *épaulement* drawings convey the principles that ensure beauty of line and facilitate ease of movement.

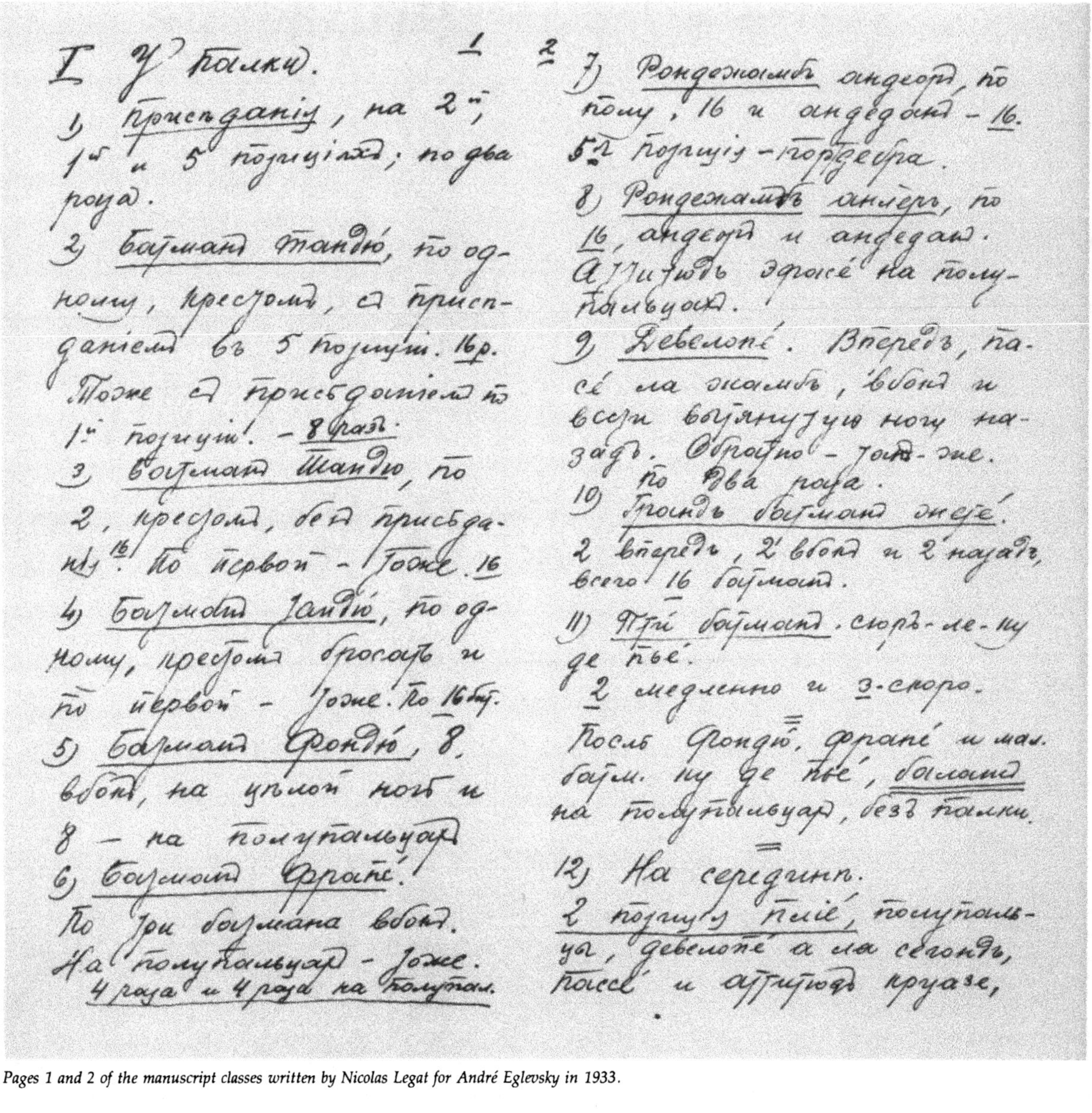

I. У палки. 1

1) приседанія, на 2-х; 1-й и 5-й позиціяхъ; по два раза.

2) батман тандю, по одному, престомъ, съ приседаніемъ въ 5 позиціи. 16 р. Тоже съ приседаніемъ по 1-й позиціи. — 8 разъ.

3) батман тандю, по 2, престомъ, безъ приседанія. 16. По первой — тоже. 16

4) батман тандю, по одному, престомъ бросать и по первой — тоже. По 16 т.

5) батман фондю, 8 вбокъ, на цѣлой ногѣ и 8 — на полупальцахъ

6) батман фрапе. По три батмана вбокъ. На полупальцахъ — тоже. 4 раза и 4 раза на полупал.

2

7) Рондежамбъ андеоръ, по тому, 16 и андеданъ — 16. 5-я позиція — пордебра.

8) Рондежамбъ анлеръ, по 16, андеоръ и андеданъ. А потомъ эфасе на полупальцахъ.

9) Девелопе. Впередъ, пасе на жамбъ, вбокъ и всегда вытянутую ногу назадъ. Обратно — тоже. По два раза.

10) Грандъ батман жете. 2 впередъ, 2 вбокъ и 2 назадъ, всего 16 батманъ.

11) Три батман. сюръ-ле-ку де пье. 2 медленно и 3 скоро.

После фондю, фрапе и мал. батм. ку де пье, батманъ на полупальцахъ, безъ палки.

12) На серединѣ.

2 позиція плие, полупальца, девелопе а ла сегондъ, пассе и аттитюдъ круазе,

Pages 1 and 2 of the manuscript classes written by Nicolas Legat for André Eglevsky in 1933.

Four Classes written by Nicolas Legat for André Eglevsky

Introductory Note:

Legat's lessons begin at the barre with *grands pliés* starting in the second position, followed by first and fifth, or fourth and fifth positions. He asks the supple student to do two *pliés* only in each position; stiffer students could do four in each position. Although Legat's combinations are always different, the general order is the same: *pliés, tendus, fondus, frappés, ronds de jambe par terre, ronds de jambe en l'air, développés, grands battements, petits battements* and some *relevés* or *batterie*. At the end of *fondu, frappé* and *petit battement* exercises, a balance is held on the *demi-pointe*. After *petit battement* he often demanded a slow turn on one leg *sur le demi-pointe* as in position for *pirouette*—this to develop balance in *pirouettes*.

Legat starts the center-work with three short *adagios* commencing from *grand plié* from the first, second, fourth or fifth positions, and ending the *enchaînement* with varied *pirouettes*. In this way, all forms of *grands* and *petits pirouettes* are introduced. This is followed by *temps liés, tendus* and other "*barre*-in-the-center" exercises with *pirouettes* and *chaînés* interspersed.

The *allegro* begins with small jumps, i.e. *glissades, assemblés, jetés, changements;* then *echappés, ballonnés, sissonnes,* intermixing with *batterie,* all performed with the accompanying *épaulement* and varied arm movements. Dance must be performed with the whole body, not just with the feet and legs.

Some examples of which I am particularly fond are:

Allegro no. 5 in the first class is typical, brilliant and difficult, done to a count of four, viz: 3 *emboîtés,* 1 *ballonné en effacé* front, and 1 *ballonné en croisé* front. It is performed from side to side, starting slowly and gradually accelerating.

Allegro no. 4 in the second class, also demanding, is done to a count of four: *brisé dessous* and *brisé dessus* twice, *coupé jeté* with *batterie, glissade jeté battu.*

Allegro no. 2 in the third class contains an *enchaînement* seldom used outside the Legat class: *failli* straight, *failli* turning in the same direction, *jeté derrière, assemblé* over.

Allegro no. 4 in the fourth class is a particularly lovely combination: *glissade,* open *cabriole en effacé* front, small *jeté, pas de basque* back and *failli.* Performed to four bars of waltz time, the step travels from side to side.

Large jumps include *grands jetés, sauts de basques, entrechats cinqs; tours en l'air* (for boys), *fouettés* (for girls), and *pirouettes en manège.*

These four classes are a guide to the class form; variations and combinations of steps are limitless. The editors have added occasional explanations to make the lessons readable by all professionals, not only those already familiar with the Legat terminology. Timing and repeats were not written by Legat but have been added to assist readers.

André Eglevsky

Class written by Nicolas Legat for André Eglevsky

Class I

BARRE-WORK

1 : Grands pliés [4/4 or 3/4]
2 *Pliés* in 2nd, 1st, and 5th positions

2 : Battements tendus [4/4]
Battement tendu with *demi-plié en croix*
16 times closing in 5th position
8 times to the side closing in 1st position

3 : Battements tendus [4/4]
2 *Battements tendus simple* in each direction *en croix*
16 times closing in 5th position
16 times to the side closing in 1st position

4 : Battements tendus jetés [4/4]
Battement tendu jeté (glissé) en croix
16 times closing in 5th position
16 times to the side closing in 1st position

5 : Battements fondus [3/4 or 4/4]
8 *Battements fondus simple* to the side
8 *Battements fondus* to the side, rising to half-toe
Hold balance *à la seconde* on half-toe

6 : Battements frappés [4/4]

&1, &2, &3,	3 *Battements frappés* to the side
&4	Hold extension

Repeat 4 times

Repeat 4 times on half-toe

7 : Ronds de jambe par terre [3/4]

16 *Ronds de jambe en dehors* finishing 5th position back
16 *Ronds de jambe en dedans* finishing 5th position front
Grand port de bras in the 5th position

8 : Ronds de jambe en l'air [2/4 or 3/4]

16 *Ronds de jambe en l'air en dehors*
16 *Ronds de jambe en l'air en dedans*
Carry working leg to *attitude en effacé*
Hold balance on half-toe

9 : Développés [3/4 *adagio*]

&a1, &a2,	
&a3,	*Développé* to the front
&a4,	*Passé*
&a1, &a2,	*Développé* to the side
&a3, &a4	Carry extended leg to *arabesque*

Repeat movement in reverse

Repeat whole sequence on half-toe

10 : Grands battements [4/4 *alla marcia*]

2 *Grands battements* in each position, *en croix*

Repeat whole sequence

11 : Petits battements [4/4 *alla marcia*]

&1, &2,	2 *Petits battements*
&3, &4	3 *Petits battements*

Repeat sequence 4 times on flat foot, and 3 times on half-toe

Hold balance *sur le cou-de-pied* on half-toe

CENTER-WORK

12 : Adage No. 1 [24 bars of 3/4 or 4/4]

1, 2,	*Grand plié* in 2nd position
3, 4,	Rise

5, 6,	Press up to half-toe
7, 8,	Lower heels
1, 2, 3, 4,	*Développé* to the side
5, 6, 7, 8,	*Passé,* and extend *attitude en croisé* back
1, 2,	*Tombé en effacé* forward to 4th position
3, 4,	*Pirouette* en dedans, sur le cou-de-pied*
5, 6, 7, 8	Finish 4th position forward, *plié en avant,* arms above head
	Repeat twice on each side

13 : Adage No. 2 [24 bars of 3/4]

1, 2,	*Grand plié* in 1st position
3, 4,	Rise
5, 6, 7,	Press up to half-toe
8,	Lower heels
1, 2, 3, 4,	*Développé croisé* front
5, 6, 7, 8,	*Passé,* and extend to *arabesque effacé*
1, 2, 3,	Hold *arabesque*
4,	*Tombé croisé* to 4th position forward
5, 6, 7, 8	*Pirouette en dehors* finish in 5th position back on half-toe, both arms extended same side as back leg
	Repeat twice on each side

14 : Adage No. 3 [24 bars of 3/4]

1, 2,	*Grand plié* in 5th position
3, 4,	Rise
5, 6,	Press up to half-toe
7, 8,	Lower heels
1, 2, 3, 4,	*Développé effacé* front
5, 6, 7, 8,	*Passé,* and extend to *attitude en effacé* back
1, 2,	*Tombé croisé* forward to 4th position
3, 4,	*Pirouette en dedans*
5, 6, 7, 8	Finish in wide 4th position, *plié en avant,* arms reaching forward
	Repeat twice on each side

15 : Temps liés No. 1 [2/4 or 4/4 *moderato*]

&1, &2,	*Temps lié croisé* forward
&	*Tombé en effacé* forward
3, &4	*Pirouette en dedans sur le cou-de-pied* back
	Finish 5th position front

Repeat on other side

May be executed once on flat foot and once on half-toe

16 : Temps liés No. 2 [2/4 *moderato*]

&1, &2,	*Temps lié croisé* back
&	*Pas de basque* back
3, &a4	*Pirouette en dehors sur le cou-de-pied* back
	Finish 5th position back

Repeat on other side, and twice more

17 : Battements tendus [2/4]

&1, &2, &3,	3 *Battements tendus* to the side with *demi-plié* commencing close front
&4	Double *pirouette en dehors* finish 5th position back

Repeat on other side, and twice more

18 : Battements fondus [4/4]

1, 2, 3, 4,	*Battement fondu croisé* front
5, 6, 7, 8,	*Battement fondu croisé* back with other leg
1, 2,	*Plié en croisé*
3, 4, 5, 6,	*Fouetté en dedans* finish 5th position front in *demi-plié*
7, 8	Straighten knees

Repeat on other side, and twice more

19 : Battements frappés [4/4]

1, &a2,	3 *Battements frappés* to the side
&	*Tombé croisé* front
3, &4	*Pirouette en dedans,* arms above head
	Finish *sur le cou-de-pied en plié*

Repeat on other side, and twice more

20 : Ronds de jambe en l'air [4/4]

&1, &2,	3 *Ronds de jambe en dehors*
&	*Passé,* extend leg to *croisé en avant en plié*
3, &4	*Pirouette fouetté en dehors*
	Close 5th position back

Repeat on other side, and twice more

21 : Ronds de jambe en l'air [4/4]

&1, &2,	3 *Ronds de jambe en dedans*
&	*Tombé effacé* front
3, &4	*Pirouette en attitude en dedans*
	Continue on other side by extending working leg *á la seconde*
	Repeat twice more

22 : Petits battements [2/4]

1, &2,	3 *Petits battements*
&3,	*Pas de basque* forward
&4,	2 *Pirouettes en dehors*
1, &2, &3,	3 *Chaînés*
&4	Step side on leading leg, other leg *sur le cou-de-pied*
	Repeat on other side, and twice more

23 : Allegro No. 1 [2/4]

	Stand 5th position *en croisé*
&1,	*Glissade derrière*
&2,	*Assemblé* over
&3,	*Failli* forward
&	*Coupé* under
a4	*Pas de basque* forward
	Repeat twice on each side

24 : Allegro No. 2 [2/4]

	Stand 5th position *en croisé*
&1,	*Glissade derrière*
&2,	*Petit jeté derrière*
&	*Coupé* under
3,	*Ballonné en effacé* forward
&4,	*Sissonne tombé en effacé* forward
&1,	*Coupé* under
&2,	*Assemblé* under
&3, &4	*Échappé battu*
	Repeat twice on each side

25 : Allegro No. 3 [2/4]

Stand *en croisé,* weight on forward leg, other foot pointed behind, with knee bent (knee to knee)

1,	*Coupé* under
&2,	*Jeté battu*
3, &4,	Repeat movement
1,	*Coupé* under
&2,	*Glissade devant*
&3, &	*Piqué pirouette en écarté en dedans*
4	Finish *tombé* forward, other foot *sur le cou-de-pied* behind

Repeat twice on each side

26 : Allegro No. 4 [4/4]

	Stand 5th position *en croisé*
1, &2,	2 *Sissonnes fermés en effacé* forward
&3,	*Sissonne fermé en effacé* back
&	*Entrechat quatre*
4	*Royale*

Repeat twice on each side

27 : Allegro No. 5 [2/4]

	Stand 5th position *en croisé*
1, &2,	3 *Emboîtés*
&3,	*Ballonné en effacé* forward
&4	*Ballonné en croisé* forward

Repeat twice on each side, accelerating

28 : Grands sauts [3/4]

	Stand 5th position *en croisé*
&1,	*Glissade derrière*
&2,	*Grand jeté en arabesque*
&	*Coupé* under
3,	*Ballonné passé* back
&4	*Petit jeté*

Repeat twice on each side

29 : Petits changements [4/4]

	Stand 5th position *en croisé*
&1,	2 *Petits changements*
&2,	*Entrechat six*
&3,	*Sissonne fermé en croisé* back
&	*Sissonne tombé en croisé* forward

4	*Assemblé fermé en croisé* back
	Repeat twice on each side

30 : Petits changements [4/4]

	Stand 5th position *en croisé*
1 to 7,	7 *Changements* turning slowly in a circle *en dehors*
&8	2 quick *entrechats quatre*
	Repeat twice on each side
	Révérence

*Note: *Pirouettes:* The general rule for *pirouettes* is that the working leg is lifted to the *sur le cou-de-pied* position in front. When *sur le cou-de-pied* back, or any other position, is required, it will be specifically stated.

In *fouettés-pirouettes* the working leg is lifted to mid-shin or mid-calf.

In *pointe*-work the girls may turn with the foot lifted to below the knee.

In *manège-pirouettes* the lifted foot is held behind the ankle, the calf muscles of each leg being held together.

These careful placings of the working leg in *pirouettes* are stylistic refinements of Legat's teaching.

Class written by Nicolas Legat for André Eglevsky

Class II

BARRE-WORK

1 : Grands pliés [4/4]

2 *Pliés* with *relevés* to half-toe in 2nd, lst, and 5th positions

2 : Battements tendus [4/4]

&a1, &a2,	2 *Battements tendus simple* to the side
&3, &4	3 *Battements tendus jetés (glissé)* to the side
	Repeat 4 times closing in 5th position
	Repeat 4 times closing in 1st position, accelerating

3 : Battements fondus [4/4]

&a1, &a2,	2 *Battements fondus* to the side
&a3, &a4,	
&1, &2, &3,	3 *Battements frappés* to the side
&4	Hold in extension
	Repeat twice on flat foot
	Repeat twice rising to half-toe

4 : Ronds de jambe par terre [2/4]

&a1, &a2,	3 *Ronds de jambe en dehors*
&a3,	*Plié* in 1st position with 3rd *rond de jambe*
&4	Extend working leg front, and continue
	Repeat sequence 4 times *en dehors*

5 : Ronds de jambe par terre [2/4]

Repeat same sequence 4 times *en dedans*

6 : Ronds de jambe en l'air [4/4 *alla marcia*]

&	Extend working leg to the side
a1, &2,	3 *Ronds de jambe en dehors*
&a	Carry working leg to 4th position *devant en plié*
3, &4,	*Fouetté en dehors*
&	Open again to side and continue movement

Repeat 4 times, twice on flat foot, and twice on half-toe

Hold balance *en attitude derrière* on half-toe

7 : Ronds de jambe en l'air [4/4 *alla marcia*]

Repeat whole sequence *en dedans*

Hold balance *en attitude devant* on half-toe

8 : Développés [3/4 *adagio*]

&a1, &2, &3,	*Développé* to the side
&a4,	*Passé*
&1, &2,	*Développé* to the back
&3,	*Plié*
&a4	*Relevé* to half-toe

Repeat sequence in reverse

Repeat both ways on half-toe

9 : Grands battements [4/4 *alla marcia*]

&a1, &2,	1 *Grand battement* front
&a3, &4,	1 *Grand battement* side
&a1, &2,	1 *Grand battement* back
&a3, &4	1 *Grand battement* side

Repeat sequence 4 times

10 : Petits battements [4/4]

&a1, &a2,	2 *Petits battements*
&a3,	2 *Petits battements* in double time
&4	Hold

Repeat sequence 4 times on flat foot, and 4 times on half-toe

Hold balance *sur le cou-de-pied* on half-toe

CENTER-WORK

11 : Adage No. 1 [24 bars of 6/8]

1, 2,	*Grand plié* in 2nd position
3, 4,	Quick rise to half-toe
5, 6, 7,	Hold
8,	Lower heels
1, 2, 3, 4,	*Développé croisé* front, arms above head
5, 6, 7, 8,	*Passé,* and extend to *arabesque croisé,* arm of supporting leg forward
1, 2,	*Plié, soutenu en dedans*
3, 4,	*Plié,* and *pirouette en dehors* from 5th position
5, 6, 7, 8	Finish 4th position *croisé* back, with *plié* on front leg
	Finishing arm positions may be varied by the individual

Repeat twice on each side

12 : Adage No. 2 [24 bars of 3/4]

1, 2,	*Grand plié* in 1st position
3, 4,	Rise to half-toe
5, 6,	Hold
7, 8,	Lower heels
1, 2, 3, 4,	*Développé* to the side, arms to opposite side
5, 6, 7,	*Passé,* and *développé en attitude effacé*
8,	Extend to *allongée*
1, 2	*Tombé* to 4th position *croisé* forward
3, 4,	*Pirouette en dedans,* both arms above head
5, 6, 7, 8	Finish 4th position, *plié* on front leg, both arms back

Repeat twice on each side

13 : Adage No. 3 [16 bars of 4/4]

1, 2,	*Grand Plié* in 5th position
3, 4,	Quick rise to half-toe, and hold
5, 6, 7, 8,	*Développé effacé* front, both arms forward
1, 2, 3,	*Tombé en arabesque effacé, en plié*
&4,	*Coupé* under, and *tombé en effacé* forward
5, 6,	*Pirouette en dedans,* both arms to shoulders
7, 8	Finish 5th position half-toe, both arms open to the side

Repeat twice on each side

14 : Temps liés [2/4]

	Stand 5th position *croisé*
&1, &2,	*Temps lié croisé* forward
&3, &4,	*Temps lié croisé* back
&1,	*Tombé en effacé* forward
&2, &3,	*Pirouette en dedans,* finish 5th position on half-toe
&4	Lower heels and *demi-plié*
	Repeat on other side, and twice more

15 : Battements jetés [2/4]

1, &2,	3 *Battements tendus jetés* to the side, first one closing front
&	*Demi-plié* in 5th position
3, &4	*Pirouette en dehors* finishing 5th position back
	Repeat on other side, and twice more

16 : Battements fondus [4/4]

&1, &2,	*Battement fondu croisé* front
&3, &4,	*Battement fondu croisé* back with other leg
&1,	*Plié en croisé*
2,	*Pirouette fouetté en dedans*
3,	Close 5th position front with *demi-plié*
4	Straighten legs
	Repeat on other side, and twice more

17 : Battements frappés [2/4]

	Stand *en face* front leg *sur le cou-de-pied*
1, &2,	2 *Battements frappés* side
&	*Tombé* forward
3,	*Coupé* under
&4,	*Pas de basque* forward
1, 2,	*Pirouette en dehors sur le cou-de-pied* back
3,	Finish *demi-plié* on one leg
4	*Coupé* under
	Repeat on other side, and twice more

18 : Ronds de jambe en l'air [3/4]

	Stand 5th position *en face*
&1, &2, &3,	3 *Ronds de jambe en l'air en dehors*
&4,	*Passé* and extend working leg forward *en plié*
1, 2, 3,	*Fouetté en dehors,* finishing *attitude croisé*

&4	Close 5th position back
	Repeat other side, and twice more

19 : Ronds de jambe en l'air [3/4]

	Stand 5th position *en face*
&1, &2, &3,	3 *Ronds de jambe en dedans*
&4,	*Passé* and extend working leg back *en plié*
1, 2, 3,	*Fouetté en dedans* finishing *attitude croisé* front
&4	Close 5th position front
	Repeat on other side, and twice more

20 : Petits battements [2/4]

	Stand 5th position *croisé*
&a1, &2,	3 *Petits battements* finishing in *demi-plié*
&a3,	*Pas de basque* forward
&4,	*Sissonne en tournant en dehors,* finishing *tombé en effacé* forward
&a1, &2,	3 *Chaînés*
&	*Tombé en effacé* forward
3, &4	*Pirouette en attitude en dedans* finishing in *attitude effacé*
	Repeat on other side, and twice more

21 : Allegro No. 1 [2/4]

	Stand 5th position *croisé*
&a1,	*Assemblé* over
&2,	2 *Entrechats quatre*
&a3,	*Sissonne tombé croisé* forward
&4	*Glissade derrière*
	Repeat other side, and twice more

22 : Allegro No. 2 [6/4]

	Stand 5th position *croisé*
&1,	*Glissade derrière*
&2,	*Jeté derrière*
&3,	*Failli* forward
&4,	*Brisé* over
&5,	*Entrechat quatre*
&6	2 *Royales*
	Repeat in same direction, *en diagonal*

Repeat on other side

23 : Allegro No. 3 [6/8]

	Stand 5th position *croisé*
1, &2, 3, &4,	2 *Échappés battus*
&5,	2 *Changements de pieds*
&6	*Entrechat six*

Repeat 4 times

24 : Allegro No. 4 [2/4]

	Stand 5th position *croisé*
&1, &2, &3, &4,	2 *Brisés volés dessus* and *dessous*
1,	*Coupé* under
&2,	*Petit jeté battu*
&3,	*Glissade derrière*
&4	*Petit jeté battu*

Repeat on other side, and twice more

25 : Grands sauts (1) [3/4 *waltz*]

	Stand 4th position *croisé*, back foot stretched behind
&a1,	*Pas de bourrée couru en effacé*
&a2,	*Grand assemblé croisé* forward
3,	*Sissonne ouvert* to the side with front leg
&a	*Coupé* under
4	*Jeté battu* to the side

Repeat other side, and twice more

26 : Grands sauts (2) [4/4]

	Stand 5th position *croisé*
&1, &2, &3, &4,	*Ballottés en effacé* forward and back twice
&1,	*Coupé* under
&2,	*Ballonné en effacé* forward
&3, &	*Pirouette piqué en dedans*
4	*Tombé croisé* forward, other leg *sur le cou-de-pied* back

Repeat on other side, and twice more

27 : Grands sauts (3) [3/4]

Stand *en croisé,* weight on forward leg, other foot pointed behind, with knee bent

&a1,	*Pas de bourrée couru en effacé*
&a2,	*Grand jeté en attitude croisé*
&3,	*Soutenu en dedans*
&4	*Failli* forward

Repeat on other side, and twice more

28 : Grands sauts (4) [4/4]

Stand weight on back leg, front leg pointed 4th position *croisé*

&	Pass weight to front leg
a1,	*Glissade derrière*
&a2,	*Entrechat cinq de volé*
&3,	*Entrechat six*
&a4	*Échappé battu* (beat front, back)

Repeat on other side, and twice more

29 : Petits changements [2/4]

Stand 5th position croisé

1 to 7,	*7 Changements de pieds* turning *en dehors* in a circle
8	Hold *demi-plié*

Repeat 4 times

30 : Grands battements [2/4]

Stand 5th position *en face*

&1, &2	*Grand battement* to the side with alternate leg

4 times travelling back, 4 times travelling forward

Révérence

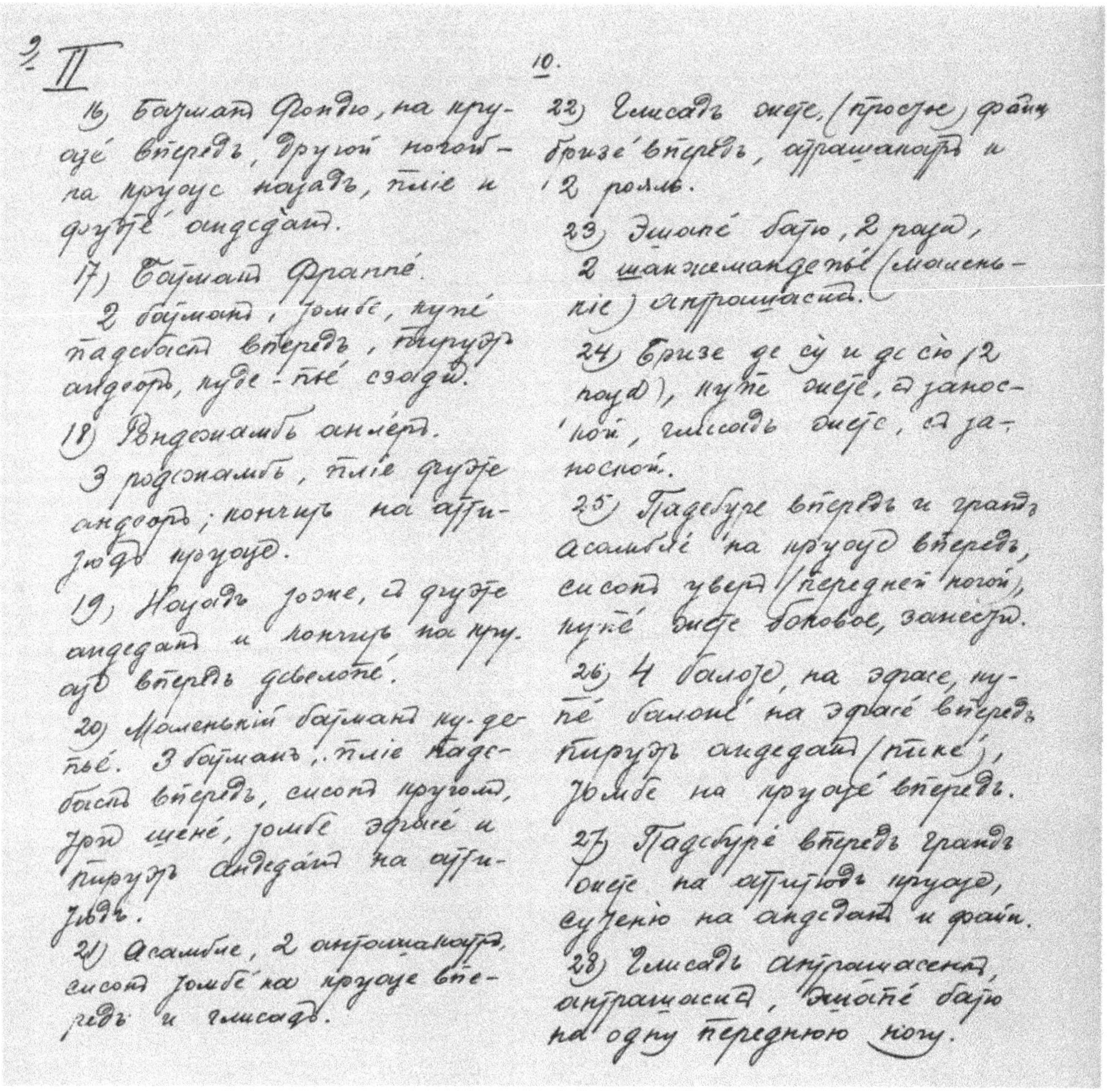

9. II

16) Батман фондю, на кру-
азе впередъ, другой ногой-
на круазе назадъ, плие и
фуэте андедан.

17) Батман фраппе.
2 батмана, томбе, купе
падебаскъ впередъ, тирбушонъ
андеоръ, купе-пике сзади.

18) Ронджамбъ анлеръ.
3 ронджамба, плие фуэте
андеоръ; кончить на атти-
тюдъ круазе.

19) Назадъ тоже, съ фуэте
андедан и кончить на кру-
азе впередъ девелоппе.

20) Маленький батман ку-де-
пье. 3 батмана, плие паде-
баскъ впередъ, сиссонъ кругомъ,
тръ шене, томбе эфасе и
тирбушонъ андедан на атти-
тюдъ.

21) Асамбле, 2 антраша катръ,
сиссонъ томбе на круазе впе-
редъ и глиссадъ.

10.

22) Глиссадъ эфасе, (просто) фаи
бризе впередъ, антраша катръ и
2 роял.

23) Эшапе батю, 2 раза,
2 шанжемандепье (малень-
кие) антраша сиз.

24) Бризе де су и де сю (2
раза), купе эфасе, съ занос-
кой, глиссадъ эфасе, съ за-
ноской.

25) Падебурре впередъ и грандъ
асамбле на круазе впередъ,
сиссонъ увертъ (передней ногой),
купе эфасе боковое, заносъ.

26) 4 баллоне, на эфасе, ку-
пе баллоне на эфасе впередъ
тирбушонъ андедан (пике),
томбе на круазе впередъ.

27) Падебуре впередъ грандъ
эфасе на аттитюдъ круазе,
сутеню на андедан и фаи.

28) Глиссадъ антраша сенкъ,
антраша сисъ, эшапе батю
на одну переднюю ногу.

Pages 9 and 10 of the manuscript classes written by Nicolas Legat for André Eglevsky in 1933.

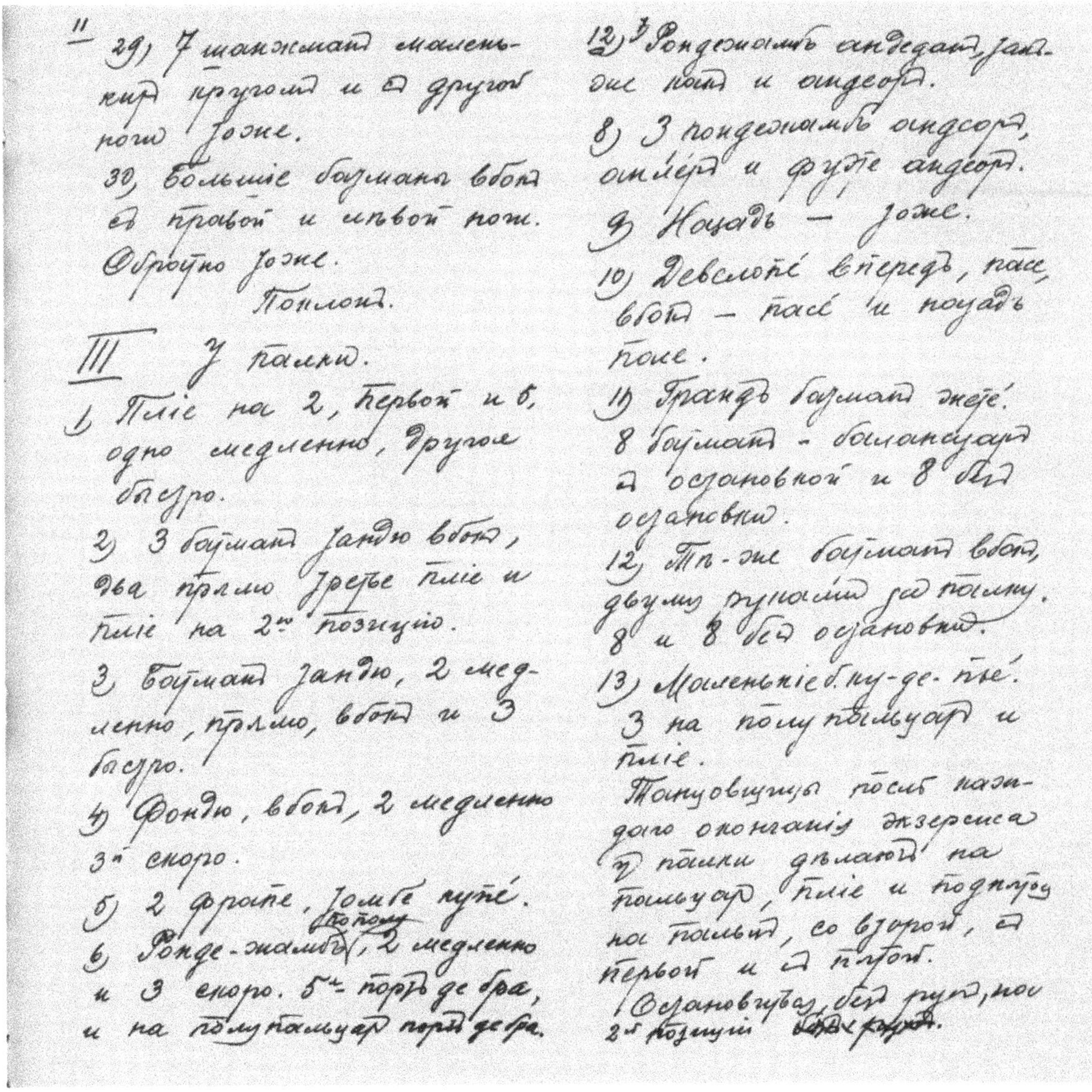

11

29) 7 шанжманъ малень-
кихъ кругомъ и съ другой
ноги тоже.
30) большие батманы вбокъ
съ правой и левой ноги.
Обратно тоже.
Поклонъ.

III У палки.

1) Плие на 2, первой и 5,
одно медленно, другое
быстро.
2) 3 батманъ тандю вбокъ,
два прямо третье плие и
плие на 2-ю позицию.
3) Батманъ тандю, 2 мед-
ленно, прямо, вбокъ и 3
быстро.
4) Фондю, вбокъ, 2 медленно
3-е скоро.
5) 2 фрапе, томбе купе.
6) Ронде-жамбъ, потомъ 2 медленно
и 3 скоро. 5-ю портъ де бра,
и на полупальцахъ портъ де бра.

12) 7 Рондежамбъ андедан, так-
же котъ и андеоръ.
8) 3 ронде жамбъ андеоръ,
атитюдъ и фуэте андеоръ.
9) Назадъ — тоже.
10) Девелопе впередъ, пасе,
вбокъ — пасе и назадъ
тоже.
11) Грандъ батманъ жете.
8 батманъ - балансуаръ
съ остановкой и 8 безъ
остановки.
12) То-же батманъ вбокъ,
двумя руками за палку.
8 и 8 безъ остановки.
13) Маленькие б. пу-де-пье.
3 на полупальцахъ и
плие.
Танцовщицы после каж-
даго окончания экзерсиса
у палки делаютъ на
пальцахъ, плие и подниму
на пальцы, со второй, съ
первой и съ пятой.
Останавливаясь безъ рукъ, на
2-й позиции.

Pages 11 and 12 of the manuscript classes written by Nicolas Legat for André Eglevsky in 1933.

Class written by Nicolas Legat for André Eglevsky

Class III

BARRE-WORK

1 : Grands pliés [3/4 or 4/4]

&1, &2,	*Grand plié* in 2nd position
&3, &4,	Rise slowly to straight legs
&1, &2,	*Grand plié* and rise quickly
&3, &4	Hold

Repeat sequence

Repeat twice in 1st and 5th positions

2 : Battements tendus [2/4 or 4/4]

&a1, &a2,	2 *Battements tendus simple* to the side
&a3,	1 *Battement tendu* with *demi-plié* in 5th position
&a4	1 *Battement tendu* with *demi-plié* in 2nd position
	Continue movement from *tendu* in 2nd position

Repeat 4 times

3 : Battements tendus jetés [4/4]

&a1, &a2,	2 *Battements tendus simple* to the side
&a3, &a4	3 *Battements tendus jetés*

Repeat 4 times closing in 5th position

Repeat 4 times closing in 1st position, accelerating

4 : Battements fondus [5/4]

&a1, &a2,	2 *Battements fondus* to the side
&a3, &a4,	
&5	1 *Battement fondu* quick

Repeat again, and twice more on half-toe

Change legs to hold balance *sur le cou-de-pied* on half-toe

5 : Battements frappés [4/4]

&1, &2,	2 *Battements frappés* to the side
&3,	*Tombé*
&4	*Coupé*

Repeat 4 times on flat foot, and twice on half-toe

Hold balance *à la seconde*

6 : Ronds de jambe par terre [2/4 or 4/4]

&a1, &a2,	2 *Ronds de jambe en dehors* slow
&a3, &a4	3 *Ronds de jambe en dehors* quick

Repeat movement 4 times

Close 5th position front

Grand Port de bras in 5th position on half-toe

7 : Rond de jambe par terre [2/4 or 4/4]

Repeat *Ronds de jambe* sequence *en dedans*

Repeat *Port de bras*

8 : Ronds de jambe en l'air [4/4]

&a1, &a2,	3 *Ronds de jambe en l'air en dehors*
&a	*Passé, plié* to 4th position *devant en l'air*
3, &a4	*Fouettés en dehors*

Continue movement without close of leg twice on flat foot, once on half-toe

Balance *en tire-bouchon*

9 : Ronds de jambe en l'air [4/4]

Repeat the same sequence *en dedans*

10 : Développés [3/4 or 4/4 *adagio*]

1, 2, 3,	*Développé* to the front
4,	*Passé*
1, 2, 3,	*Développé* to the side
4,	*Passé*
1, 2, 3, 4,	*Développé* to the back and hold *arabesque*

1, 2, 3, 4	Lower working leg slowly to 5th position

Repeat in reverse commencing from the back

Repeat whole sequence on half-toe

11 : Grands Battements [4/4 *alla marcia*]

	Grands battements balançoire forward and back
1 to 16	8 times with stop
1 to 8	8 times without stopping
	Grands battements balançoire to the side alternate legs, facing *barre*
1 to 16	8 times with stop
1 to 8	8 times without stopping

12 : Petits battements [4/4]

&a1, 2, 3,	3 *Petits battements* accent front, 3rd one *en plié*
&4,	*Relevé* and change working leg to *sur le cou-de-pied* back
&a1, 2, 3,	3 *Petits battements* accent back, 3rd one *en plié*
&4	*Relevé* and change working leg to *sur le cou-de-pied* front

Repeat sequence, and again on half-toe

Hold balance *sur le cou-de-pied* on half-toe, arms down as for *pirouette*

CENTER-WORK

13 : Adage No. 1 [16 bars of 4/4]

1, 2,	*Grand plié* in 4th position *effacé*
3, 4,	Rise
5, 6, 7, 8,	Lift leg *en l'air* to *arabesque effacé*
1, 2, 3, 4,	*Passé* and *developpé croisé* front
5,	*Tombé croisé* forward
6, 7, 8	*Pirouette en dedans* finishing 5th position half-toe with both arms above head

Repeat twice on each side

14 : Adage No. 2 [24 bars of 3/4]

1, 2,	*Grand plié* in 1st position
3, 4,	Rise quickly to 5th position half-toe, both arms above head
5, 6, 7, 8,	*Développé* to the side

1, 2, 3, 4,	*Passé* and extend working leg to *attitude croisé*
5, 6,	*Tombé effacé* forward
7, 8,	*Pirouette en dedans sur le cou-de-pied* finish on one leg *en plié*
1, 2, 3, 4,	Open working leg to side and gather *soutenu en dedans*
5, 6, 7, 8	Finish 5th position *en plié,* and straighten knees

Repeat twice on each side

15 : Adage No. 3 [24 bars of 4/4]

1, 2,	*Grand plié* in 5th position
3, 4,	Rise
5, 6, 7, 8,	Press up to half-toe with front leg *sur le cou-de-pied,* front arm waist level, back arm above head
1, 2, 3, 4,	*Développé effacé* front
5, 6, 7, 8,	Brush leg through 1st position, turning to *attitude effacé* on half-toe
1, 2,	*Tombé croisé* forward
3, 4,	*Pirouette en dehors*
5, 6, 7, 8	Finish in wide 4th position back, *plié* on front leg, arms forward

Repeat twice on each side

16 : Temps liés [2/4]

	Stand 5th position *croisé*
&1, &2,	*Temps lié en effacé* forward
&3, &4,	*Temps lié en croisé* forward
&1,	*Tombé en effacé* forward
2, 3,	*Pirouette en dedans*
&4	Finish 5th position front in *demi-plié*

Repeat on other side

Repeat twice on half-toe

17 : Temps liés [2/4]

	Stand 5th position *croisé*
&1, &2,	*Temps lié en effacé* back
&3, &4,	*Temps lié en croisé* back
&1,	*Pas de basque en arrière*
2, 3,	*Pirouette en dehors*
&4	Finish 5th position back in *demi-plié*

Repeat on other side

Repeat twice on half-toe

18 : Battements tendus [4/4]

	Stand 5th position *en face*
1 to 4,	4 *Battements tendus* to the side, closing 5th position back, front, back, front
1, 2,	*Flic en dedans* with back leg to *sur le cou-de-pied* front
3, 4	Close 5th position front in *demi-plié*
	Repeat on other side
	Repeat twice with double turn on the *flic*

19 : Battements fondus [3/4]

	Stand 5th position *croisé*
&1, &a2,	*Battement fondu effacé* front
&a	*Tombé en effacé* forward
3, &a	Slow turn *en dedans en arabesque*
4	Close *arabesque* leg to *sur le cou-de-pied* front
	Repeat on other side
	Repeat on half-toe

20 : Battements frappés and ronds de jambe en l'air [4/4]

	Stand 5th position *en face*
&a1, &2,	3 *Battements frappés* to the side
&a3, &a4,	2 *Ronds de jambe en l'air en dehors*
&a1,	*Passé* to 4th position *croisé* front *en l'air*
2,	*Fouetté en dehors*
3,	Close 5th position back in *demi-plié*
&4	Straighten knees
	Repeat on other side
	Repeat twice on half-toe

21 : Battements frappés and ronds de jambe en l'air [4/4]

Repeat the sequence 4 times in reverse commencing with back leg; the *ronds de jambe* and *fouettés* will be executed *en dedans*

22 : Petits battements [3/4 *mazurka*]

	Stand 5th position *croisé;* place front foot *sur le cou-de-pied;* travel diagonally
1, 2, 3, 4, 5, 6,	2 slow *petits battements*
1, 2, 3,	3 quick *petits battements*

4, 5, 6,	3 quick *chainé* turns
1, 2, 3,	*Tombé en effacé* forward
4, 5, 6,	*Pas de bourrée* under to 4th position *croisé*
1, 2, 3, 4, 5, 6	*Pirouette en attitude en dehors* finish *croisé*
	Quick *coupé* under to commence other side
	Repeat 4 times

23 : Allegro No. 1 [1 bar 3/4, 1 bar 4/4]

	Stand 5th position *croisé*
&a1,	*Glissade derrière*
&2,	*Coupé* under
&3,	*Assemblé* under
1, &2,	*Echappé battu* in 2nd position, finish front leg *sur le cou-de-pied* back
&3,	*Coupé* under
&a4	*Pas de basque* forward
	Repeat on other side, and twice more

24 : Allegro No. 2 [3/4 *waltz moderato,* or 2/4]

	Stand 5th position *croisé*
&a1,	*Failli en avant*
&a2,	*Failli en tournant en dedans* (using same leg)
&a3,	*Glissade derrière*
&	*Jeté derrière*
a4	*Assemblé* over
	Repeat other side, and twice more

25 : Allegro No. 3 [4/4 *alla marcia*]

	Stand 5th position *croisé*
&a1, &a2,	2 *Changements de pieds*
&a3,	*Entrechat six*
&a4	*Sissonne fermé en avant croisé*
	Repeat other side, and twice more

26 : Allegro No. 4 [3/4 *mazurka*]

	Stand 5th position *croisé*
1, 2, 3,	*Pas de basque* forward closing 5th position
4, 5, 6,	*Pas de basque* back with back leg closing 5th position
1,	*Sissonne ouvert* to the side with back leg
2,	*Coupé* under

3,	*Ballonné passé* back
4, 5,	*Jeté devant* to the side
6	*Petit sissonne sur le cou-de-pied* front
	Repeat other side, and twice more

27 : Allegro No. 5 [3/4 *waltz*]

	Stand 5th position *croisé*
&a1,	*Glissade derrière*
&2,	*Entrechat cinq derrière sur le cou-de-pied* back
&a3,	*Sissonne tombé en effacé* back
&	*Assemblé fermé* with front leg
a4	*Failli en avant*
	Repeat other side, and twice more

28 : Grands sauts (for men) [3/4 or 4/4]

	Stand 5th position *croisé*
1 to 8,	8 *Entrechats six*
1, 2,	Small *echappé* to 2nd position
3 to 8	*Pirouettes en dehors* finishing 5th position back
	Repeat on other side

29 : Coupé ballonné [4/4]

	Stand 5th position *croisé*
1, &2, &	*Coupé grand ballonné en effacé* forward
3,	*Coupé,* stepping slightly upstage
&4	*Ballonné en tournant en dedans*
	Repeat in series *en diagonal*
	Repeat on other side

30 : Tours en l'air [4/4]

	Stand 5th position *croisé*
&a1,	2 small *changements de pieds*
&2	*Tour en l'air* (double for boys)
	Repeat alternate legs

31 : Petits changements [2/4]

Stand 5th position *en face*
16 small *changements de pieds*

Révérence

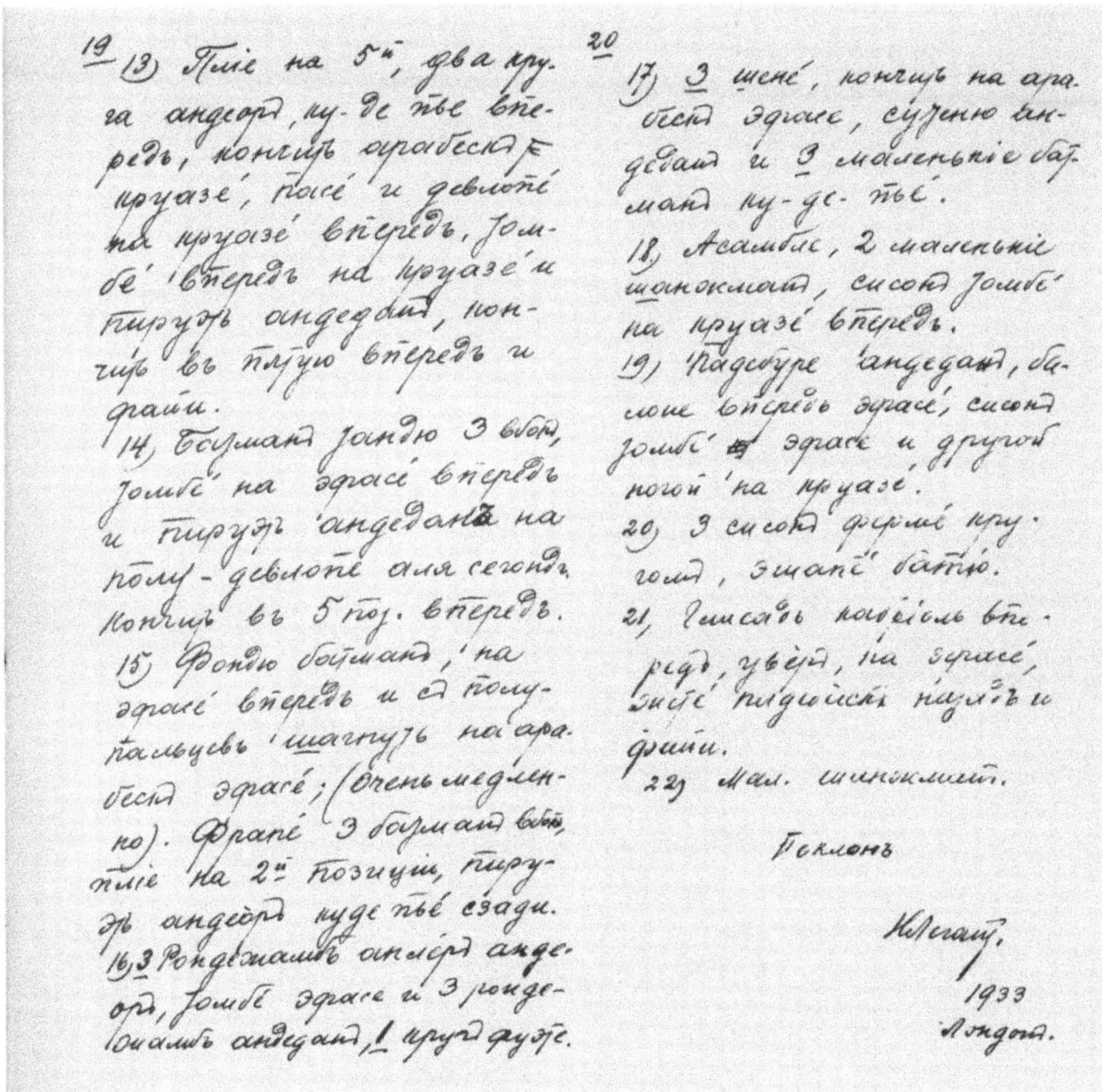

Pages 19 and 20 of the manuscript classes written by Nicolas Legat for André Eglevsky in 1933.

Class written by Nicolas Legat for André Eglevsky

Class IV

BARRE-WORK

1 : Grands pliés [3/4 or 4/4]

2 *Pliés* in 2nd, 1st, 4th, and 5th positions

2 : Battements tendus [2/4]

2 *Battements tendus* with *demi-plié* in each direction *en croix* with arm movements as follows: carry arm forward and above head with forward *tendus,* open to the side with *tendus* to the side, lower and carry forward to *arabesque* with *tendus* to the back, and open again to the side with *tendus* to the side

The arm should describe one continuous flowing movement

3 : Battements tendus jetés [4/4]

&1, &	3 *Battements tendus jetés* to the side
2	Close 3rd *tendu* with *demi-plié*

Repeat 16 times

4 : Battements fondus [3/4 or 4/4]

&1, &2,	*Battement fondu* to the side
&3, &4	*Demi-plié* in extended position *(fondu doublé)*

Repeat 8 times

Hold balance *sur le cou-de-pied* on half-toe with arms above head

5 : Battements frappés [2/4]

&1, &2	3 *Battements frappés* to the side

Repeat 16 times

Hold balance in low *à la seconde* on half-toe with arms above head

6 : Ronds de jambe [6/4]

&1, &2, &3,	3 *Ronds de jambe par terre en dehors*
&4, &5, &6	3 *Ronds de jambe en l'air en dehors*

Repeat 4 times

Finish with *développé* on half-toe to the front with both arms above head

7 : Ronds de jambe [6/4]

Repeat *ronds de jambe* sequence *en dedans*

Finish in *arabesque* on half-toe both arms forward

8 : Développés [4/4 *adagio*]

&1, &2,	*Développé* to the side
3, & 4,	Carry leg to the back
&1, &2,	Return leg to the side
3, &4	Close 5th position

Repeat on half-toe

9 : Grands Battements [4/4 *alla marcia*]

&a1, &2	1 *Grand battement* on half-toe in each position *en croix*

Repeat 4 times

10 : Petits battements [4/4]

&1, &2,	3 *Petits battements sur le cou-de-pied* front
&3, &4	*Plié* and *fouetté en dehors*

Repeat sequence from *sur le cou-de-pied* back with *fouetté en dedans*

Repeat both ways on half-toe

Hold balance *sur le cou-de-pied* on half-toe with arms down

CENTER-WORK

11 : Adage No. 1 [3 bars of 4/4 *adagio*]

1, &2,	*Grand plié* in 2nd position
&3, &4,	*Pirouette en dedans en attitude* from depth of *plié,* finishing *en croisé*

1, &2,	*Passé*
&3, &4,	*Développé effacé* front
&1,	*Tombé en effacé* forward to 4th position
&2, &3,	*Pirouette en dedans*
&4	Finish in 4th position on half-toe with both arms back
	Repeat twice on each side

12 : Adage No. 2 [3 bars of 4/4 *adagio*]

1, &2,	*Grand plié* in 1st position
&3, &4,	Single *pirouette en dehors en attitude* from depth of *plié* finishing *en croisé*
1, &2, &3,	*Développé* to the side
4,	*Tombé en croisé* forward to 4th position
1, &	*Pirouette en dehors*
2,	Finish *tombé en croisé* forward
3,	*Pirouette en dehors*
&4	Finish 4th position *croisé* back, arms to the side
	Repeat twice on each side.

13 : Adage No. 3 [4 bars of 4/4 *adagio*]

1, &2,	*Grand plié* in 5th position
3, &4,	Double *pirouette en dehors sur le cou-de-pied* front, from depth of *plié*
1, &2,	Finish *en arabesque croisé*
3, &4,	*Passé*
1, 2, 3,	*Développé croisé* front
4,	*Tombé en croisé* in 4th position
1, &2,	*Pirouette en dedans*
3, &4	Finish 5th position front and *failli*
	Repeat twice on each side

14 : Battements tendus [4/4]

&1, &2, &3,	3 *Battements tendus* to the side closing front, back, front
4,	*Tombé en effacé* front
1, &2,	*Pirouette en dedans*
3, &4	Finish *développé* to the side and hold
	Continue on other side, and repeat twice more

15 : Battements fondus [4/4 *allegro*]

1, &2,	*Battement fondu effacé* front on half-toe
3, &4,	Step *en arabesque* half-toe (slow movement)

1, &2,	3 *Battements frappés* to the side
&	*Demi-plié* in 2nd position
3, &4	*Pirouette en dehors sur le cou-de-pied* back
	Pass foot to *sur le cou-de-pied* front, and repeat on other side
	Repeat sequence twice more

16 : Ronds de jambe en l'air [4/4]

1, &a2,	3 *Ronds de jambe en l'air en dehors*
&	*Tombé en effacé* front in 4th position
a3, &a4	3 *Ronds de jambe en l'air en dedans* rotating
	Continue movement on the other side from the *en l'air* position
	Repeat sequence twice more

17 : Chainés en diagonal [4/4]

&1, &2,	3 *Chainés* finishing in
3, &4,	*Arabesque effacé en demi-plié*
&1, &2,	*Soutenu en dedans*
3, &4	3 *Petits battements sur le cou-de-pied en écarté*
	Continue series in same direction
	Repeat on other side

18 : Allegro No. 1 [4/4 *alla marcia*]

&a1,	2 *Petits changements*
&2	*Sissonne tombé en croisé* front
	Continue by closing leg behind with first jump
	Repeat sequence 8 times

19 : Allegro No. 2 [4/4]

&a1,	*Pas de bourrée en tournant en dedans*
&a2,	*Ballonné en effacé* front
&a3,	*Sissonne tombé en effacé* front
&a 4	*Sissonne tombé* with other leg *en croisé* front
	Repeat other side, and twice more

20 : Allegro No. 3 [4/4]

&1, &2, &3,	3 *Sissonnes fermés* moving in a circle
&4	*Echappé battu* in double time

Repeat other side, and twice more

21 : Allegro No. 4 [3/4]

&1,	*Glissade derrière*
&a2,	*Cabriole ouvert en effacé* front
&	*Petit jeté* (over)
a3,	*Pas de basque* back
&a4	*Failli*

Repeat on other side, and twice more

22 : Petits changements [2/4]

16 *Petits changements*

Révérence

Class remembered by Alan Carter

Class V

BARRE-WORK

1 : Grands pliés [*waltz, moderato e legato*]

2 *Grands pliés* with rise to *demi-pointe* in 2nd, 1st, and 5th positions both sides, arm carried to the side through *bras-bas*

2 : Battements tendus with demi-plié [2/4 *moderato*]

&1, &2,	2 *Battements tendus* front
&3, &4	*Demi-plié* in 5th position

Repeat movement *en croix* with arm *de côté*

Repeat *enchaînement* in 1st position to the side, arm *en bas*

3 : Battements tendus [2/4 *allegretto*]

&1, &2, &3,	3 *Battements tendus de côté* in 5th position
&4,	Wait
&5, &6, &7, &8,	2 *Battements tendus en avant*
&1, &2, &3,	3 *Battements tendus de côté*
&4,	Wait
&5, &6, &7, &8	2 *Battements tendus en arrière*

Repeat whole sequence

Repeat 4 times *de côté* in 1st position, arm *en bas*

4 : Battements tendus jetés [2/4 *allegretto*]

&1,	*Battement tendu jeté en avant,* right leg closing 5th
&2,	*Battement tendu jeté de côté,* right leg
&3,	*Battement tendu jeté en arrière,* right leg
&4,	*Battement tendu jeté en avant,* left leg
&5,	*Battement tendu jeté en arrière,* right leg
&6,	*Battement tendu jeté de côté,* right leg
&7,	*Battement tendu jeté en avant,* right leg
&8	*Battement tendu jeté en arrière,* left leg

1 to 8	Repeat sequence
&1, &2, &3,	3 *Battements tendus jetés de côté,* right leg closing 1st position
&4,	1 *Battement tendu jeté de côté,* left leg
5 to 8	Repeat in 1st position
1 to 8	Continue with *port de bras* down to *en bas* and through front to the side
	Grand battement to the side and close 5th position front.

5 : Battements fondus [slow *waltz*]

&a1, &a2,	*Battement fondu en avant* right leg, with *port de bras,* right arm *en haut*
&a3, &a4,	*Coupé, battement fondu en arrière* left leg, arm *en arabesque*
&a5, &a6,	*Coupé, battement fondu de côté* right leg, arm *de côté*
&a7, &a8,	*Battement fondu de côté* right leg, arm *de côté*
&a1, &a2,	*Battement fondu en arrière* right leg, arm en *arabesque*
&a3, &a4,	*Coupé, battement fondu en avant* left leg, arm *en haut*
&a5, &a6,	*Coupé, battement fondu de côté* right leg, arm *de côté*
&a7, &a8	*Battement fondu de côté* right leg, arm *de côté*
	Repeat sequence with rise to *demi-pointe*
	Hold balance *sur le cou-de-pied devant,* arms *en haut*

6 : Battements frappés [3/4 *polonaise*]

1, &a2,	3 *Battements frappés de côté,* arm *de côté*
&3,	1 *Battement frappé en arrière*
4, &a5,	3 *Battements frappés de côté*
&6	1 *Battement frappé devant*
	Repeat sequence
	Repeat on *demi-pointe*
	Hold balance in finishing position

7 : Ronds de jambe par terre [*waltz*]

	Preparation from 5th position: *tendu en fondu devant* and extend stretched leg to side
1, 2,	2 *Ronds de jambe en dehors*
3, 4,	1 *Rond de jambe en dehors en fondu*
5, 6, 7,	3 *Ronds de jambe en dehors*
8	To finish side

Repeat sequence *en dedans*

Repeat *en dehors* and *en dedans* finishing 5th position front

1 to 8,	*Grand port de bras*
1 to 8	*Grand port de bras en demi-pointe*

8 : Ronds de jambe en l'air en dehors [2/4 *moderato e legato*]

	Preparation: stretch leg to side *en l'air*
1, 2, 3,	3 *Ronds de jambe en l'air en dehors*
4,	Hold extension side
5, 6, 7, 8	Carry leg *en avant* and open again to side

Repeat on *demi-pointe*

Hold balance *développé en avant* on *demi-pointe,* stretch knee, arms *en haut*

9 : Ronds de jambe en l'air en dedans [2/4]

Same sequence as for *en dehors*

Hold balance *développé arabesque à deux bras en demi-pointe*

10 : Développés [4/4 *sostenuto*]

1, 2, 3, 4,	*Développé en avant,* arm *devant*
5, 6,	Carry leg quickly to side, arm *de côté*
7, 8,	Hold side
1, 2, 3, 4, 5, 6,	*Passé, développé en attitude croisé*
7, 8,	Stretch leg behind and close 5th position
1, 2, 3, 4,	*Développé en arrière*
5, 6,	Carry leg quickly to side
7, 8,	Hold side
1, 2, 3, 4, 5, 6,	*Passé, développé effacé en avant*
7, 8	Close 5th position

Repeat on *demi-pointe*

11 : Grands battements balançoire [6/8 *marcato*]

	Preparation: *tendu* side and close 1st position, arm side *allongeé*
1, 2, 3,	*Grands battements en avant, en arrière, en avant*
4,	Close 1st position
5, 6, 7,	*Grands battements en arrière, en avant, en arrière*
8	Close 5th position

Repeat sequence 4 times

12 : Grands battements to the side (facing barre) [4/4]

	Execute in the 1st position, alternate legs
1, 2, 3,	*Grands battements* to right, to left, to right
4,	Close 1st position
1, 2, 3,	*Grands battements* to left, to right, to left
4	Close 1st position

Repeat sequence 4 times

13 : Petits battements [1 bar 4/4, 1 bar 5/4 *allegretto*]

	Preparation: *tendu* side, close *sur le cou-de-pied devant,* arm *en bas*
&1, &2, &3,	Beat back-front 3 times
4,	Hold *sur le cou-de-pied*
&1, &2, &3, &4,	Beat back-front 4 times
5	Hold *sur le cou-de-pied*

Repeat sequence 4 times on flat foot, and 4 times on *demi-pointe*

Hold balance *sur le cou-de-pied en demi-pointe,* arms *en bas.* Turn slowly to the *barre en demi-pointe.* Close 5th position

CENTER-WORK

14 : Adage No. 1 [*waltz, moderato con moto*]

1, 2, 3, 4,	*Grand plié* in 2nd position and rise
5, 6, 7, 8,	Press up to *demi-pointe,* arms *de côté*
1, 2, 3, 4,	Right leg *développé croisé en avant,* arms *en haut,* and close 5th position
5, 6, 7, 8,	Left leg *développé* side, arms *de côté*
1, 2,	*Passé*
3, 4,	*Tombé croisé en avant*
5, 6,	*Pirouette en dehors,* arms *en bas*
7, 8	Finish 5th position *en demi-pointe,* right foot *derrière,* left arm on hip, right arm *de côté* with palm facing upwards, head to left corner
	Tendu left foot to side into 2nd position

Repeat *adage* to left

Repeat to both sides with *développés en demi-pointe*

15 : Adage No. 2 [*waltz, moderato con moto*]

1, 2, 3, 4,	*Grand plié* in 1st position and rise
5, 6, 7, 8,	Press up to *demi-pointe,* arms *en haut*
1, 2, 3, 4,	Right leg *développé effacé en avant*
5, 6, 7, 8,	*Passé* and *développé attitude croisé*
1, 2, 3, 4,	*Passé,* and *tombé en effacé en avant* to 4th position
5, 6,	*Pirouette en dedans sur le cou-de-pied,* without *fouetté,* left leg *sur le cou-de-pied* front
7, 8	*Tombé* forward to finish 4th position, both arms *de côté,* palms facing upwards, head to the left

Repeat *adage* to the left

Repeat to both sides with *développés en demi-pointe*

16 : Adage No. 3 [*waltz, sostenuto e cantabile*]

1, 2, 3, 4,	*Grand plié* in 5th position, right leg in front, and rise
5, 6, 7, 8,	Press up to *demi-pointe,* right leg *sur le cou-de-pied,* left arm *en haut,* right arm *demi-bras*
1, 2, 3, 4,	Right leg *développé attitude effacé,* arms *en haut allongée*
5, 6, 7, 8,	*Tombé en croisé en avant* into *arabesque,* left arm at eye-level, right arm *de côté*
1, 2, 3, 4,	*Coupé* and *développé,* right leg *en écarté*
5, 6,	*Fondu* and *pirouette en dehors en attitude devant,* arms *en haut*
7, 8	Finish *tombé* back into 4th position *croisé,* arms *de côté,* with palms facing upwards

Repeat as previous *adages*

17 : Temps liés [6/4]

1, 2, 3,	3 *Battements tendus* side with right leg, front, back, front
4, 5, 6,	*Temps lié croisé en avant*
1, 2, 3,	*Tombé en effacé en avant*
4, 5, 6	*Pirouette sur le cou-de-pied en dedans,* arms *en bas,* finish 5th position left leg in front

Repeat with left leg, and again on each side

18 : Temps liés [6/4 *con moto*]

1, 2, 3,	3 *Battements tendus jetés* side with right leg closing front, back, front
4, 5, 6,	*Temps lié croisé en arrière*
1, 2, 3,	Right leg *tombé en effacé*
4, 5, 6	*Pirouette sur le cou-de-pied en dedans,* arms *en haut* finish 5th position left leg in front

Repeat with left leg, and again on each side

19 : Battements fondus [2/4 *adagio*]

1, 2,	Right leg *battement fondu* to the side
3, 4,	Right leg *battement fondu croisé en avant*
5,	Right leg *tombé en croisé en avant*
6, 7,	*Pirouette en attitude en dedans*
8	Finish *attitude effacé*

Repeat with left leg

Repeat both sides with *battement fondu* on *demi-pointe*

20 : Battements frappés [1 bar 4/4, 1 bar 5/4, *alla marcia*]

	Prepare right leg to the side *en l'air*
1, 2,	2 *Battements frappés* side
3, &	2 Quick *battements frappés* side
4,	*Tombé* in 2nd position *demi-plié*
5, 6,	*Pirouette en dehors*
7, 8,	Finish in *attitude croisé*
9	*Coupé* left leg to the side *en l'air*

Repeat with left leg

Repeat both sides with *battements frappés* on *demi-pointe*

21 : Ronds de jambe en l'air [*waltz vivo*]

1, 2, 3,	3 *Ronds de jambe en l'air en dehors* with right leg
4,	Hold side
5, 6,	*Passé* to *croisé en avant en fondu*
&7,	*Fouetté pirouette en dehors*
8	*Coupé*

Repeat with left leg

Repeat both sides with *ronds de jambe* on *demi-pointe*

Repeat the exercise 4 times *en dedans*

22 : Grands battements [3 bars of 2/4 *ben marcato*]

&a1, &a2,	
&a3, &a4,	*Grands battements* with right leg front, side, back
&a5, &a6	

Repeat with left leg, and again on each side

23 : Petits battements [2/4 *galop*]

Prepare right foot *sur le cou-de-pied* in front, right arm in front *demi-bras,* left arm *de côté*

&1, &2, &3,	3 *Petits battements,* back, front
4,	Hold
&5, &6, &7,	3 *Petits battements en demi-pointe*
8	Hold
&1, 2,	*Échappé* to 2nd position *demi-plié*
3, 4, 5,	*Pirouette en dehors sur le cou-de-pied en arrière*
6, 7,	Close right leg 5th position back, *demi-plié*
8	Left leg *sur le cou-de-pied* in front

Repeat to left and twice more

24 : Allegro No. 1 [6/8 *allegretto*]

&1,	*Glissade derrière* to right
&2,	*Assemblé dessus*
&3, &4	2 *Petits changements de pieds*

Repeat to left, and again both sides with *battu* finishing with *tendu* side, *demi-plié* in 2nd position, *pirouette en dehors* finishing in deep 4th position

25 : Allegro No. 2 [2/4 *allegretto e cantabile*]

&1,	*Glissade derrière to right*
&2,	*Coupé* under
&3,	*Pas de basque ouvert* to *croisé en avant*
&4,	*Pas de basque ouvert* to *croisé en arrière*
&5,	Brush front leg back into *brisé en arrière*
&6,	*Relevé tombé en effacé en avant*
7, 8	*Pirouette en dedans,* left hand on hip, right arm *en haut*

Close right leg 5th position front

Repeat on left, and twice more

26 : Grands sauts [*waltz brilliant*]

&1,	*Glissade devant* right leg front
&2,	*Ballonné effacé en avant,* right arm *en haut,* left arm *de côté*
&3,	*Jeté devant*
&4,	*Relevé tombé en croisé en avant*

5, 6, 7, *Grand pirouette relevé en dedans à la seconde,* arms *en haut*
8 Close 5th position right leg in front

Repeat commencing *glissade dessus* instead of *glissade devant*

Repeat the *enchaînment* 4 times

27 : Grands sauts [6 bars of 2/4 *giocoso*]
1, &2, &3, &4, 2 *Échappés battus (entrechat six)*
&5, 2 *Petits changements de pieds*
&6 Single *tour en l'air*

Repeat on other side

Repeat both sides with double *tour en l'air*

Révérence

Note: Alan Carter states that music time signatures, indications and counts are from memory.

Class remembered by Barbara Gregory

Class VI

BARRE-WORK

1 : Grands pliés [4 bars of 12/8; for 2 *pliés, andantino*]

1, &a2,	*Grand plié* in 2nd position
3, &a4,	Rise
1, &2,	Press up to half-toe
3, &4,	Lower to heels
1, &a2,	*Grand plié* in 2nd position
3, &a4,	Rise
1,	Press up to half-toe
&2,	Lower to heels
3, &a4	*Tendu* to close in 1st position

Repeat sequence in 1st position, and in 5th positions front and back

2 : Battements tendus [4 bars of 4/4 *andantino e legato*]

&1, &2,	2 *Battements tendus simple* to the front
&3,	1 *Battement tendu* front with *demi-plié* in 5th position
&4	Extend working leg to the side

Repeat sequence to the side closing back, front, back with *demi-plié* and extend to the back

Repeat sequence to the back and extend to the side

4 *Battements tendus simple en croix* from side extension close in front, then 1 front, 1 side, 1 back

Repeat the *enchaînment* commencing to the back

Repeat the *enchaînement* twice to the side closing in 1st position

3 : Battements tendus jetés [4 bars 2/4 *allegro*]

1, 2, 3,	3 *Battements tendus jetés* to the side
4,	Hold in 5th position
1, 2, 3, 4,	Repeat movement
1, 2,	1 *Battement tendu simple* to the front

3, 4,	1 *Battement tendu simple* to the back, with other leg
1, 2, 3,	3 *Battements tendus jetés* to the side
4	Hold in 5th position
	Repeat in reverse
	Repeat twice to the side in 1st position

4 : Battements fondus [4 bars 6/8 *moderato e molto cantabile*]

&1, &2,	*Battement fondu en effacé* front
&3, &4,	Pass with *petit battement* and *fondu en effacé* back
&1,	*Plié* in extension
&2,	Carry leg to side, straightening supporting leg
&3, &4,	Carry leg to *effacé* front and *plié*
1, 2, 3, 4	Brush leg through 1st position to *croisé* back, straightening supporting leg
	Repeat in reverse
	Repeat *enchaînement* on half-toe
	Close to 5th position on half-toe, lift back leg to *sur le cou-de-pied,* and hold balance; one hand on hip, other arm to the side

5 : Battements frappés [8 bars of 2/4 *galop moderato*]

1, 2, 3,	3 *Battements frappés en croix,* front, side, back
4,	Hold in extension back
1, 2, 3, 4,	Repeat in reverse
1, 2, 3, 4,	Repeat again as first time
1, &2,	3 quick *battements frappés* to the side from front, back, front
3, &4	*Tombé devant* and *relevé* turning *en dehors* to face other way
	Repeat other side
	Repeat sequence on half-toe
	Extend front leg and hold balance

6 : Ronds de jambe par terre [8 bars 3/4 *valse moderato*]

&1, &2, &	3 *Ronds de jambe en dehors*
3, &a4,	*Piqué* front, side, back

1 to 8,	Repeat movement twice more
&1, &a	2 *Ronds de jambe en dehors*
2, &3, &a4	*Rond de cuisse en dehors* closing 5th position back
	Repeat sequence *en dedans*

7 : Assemblé soutenu and ports de bras [16 bars 3/4 *poco meno mosso*]

Demi-plié in 5th position
Extend foot to 4th position front, *rond de jambe par terre en plié* to 4th position back, lower heel
Grand port de bras en dedans
Rond de jambe par terre en plié en dedans
Step to half-toe in 4th position
Grand port de bras en dehors
Demi-plié in 4th position and pass weight to front leg finishing in *arabesque croisé par terre*

8 : Ronds de jambe en l'air [2 bars 4/4 *moderato e molto cantabile*]

1,	*Demi-plié* in 5th position
2, 3,	*Pirouette en dehors* finishing *en demi-plié* with working leg extended *effacé* front *par terre*
&4,	Lift leg and open to the side *en l'air*
1, &2,	2 *Ronds de jambe en dehors*
&3,	Carry leg to *attitude*
4	Close 5th position back
	Repeat in reverse
	Repeat whole sequence on half-toe

9 : Développés [2 bars 12/8 *andante e cantabile*]

&1, &2,	*Développé* to the front
&3,	*Plié* in extension
&4,	Carry leg to side, straightening supporting leg
&1, &2, &3,	*Passé* to *attitude effacé,* extending leg to *allongée*
&4	Close 5th position back
	Repeat in reverse
	Repeat whole sequence on half-toe

10 : Grands battements [4 bars 4/4 *alla marcia*]

&a1, &a2, &a — 3 *Grands battements* to the front
3, — Finish third one in *demi-plié* 5th position
&4 — Stretch knees

Repeat movement *en croix* and again

11 : Petits battements [8 bars 2/4 *allegro moderato*]

&1, &2, — 2 Slow *petits battements* accent front
&3, &4, — 3 Quick *petits battements*
&1, &2, — 2 Slow *petits battements*
&3, — *Piqué effacé* front *en plié*
&4 — *Passé* with *petits battements* front, back

Repeat in reverse with accent back

Repeat whole sequence on half-toe

12 : Relevés [4 bars 4/4 *moderato con molto*]

Stand in 2nd position facing *barre*
4 *Pliés-relevés,* making *port de bras* inclining arm over head and opening again to side

Repeat movement with other arm *port de bras*

Repeat sequence making circular *port de bras* with back bend

Hold balance in 2nd position on half-toe

CENTER-WORK

13 : Adage No. 1 [16 bars of 3/4 *molto cantabile*]

1, 2, — *Grand plié* in 2nd position, arms opening to side
3, 4, — Rise, lowering arms
5, 6, 7, — Press up to half-toe, lifting arms forward and open to side
8, — *Plié en effacé,* weight on back foot, point forward leg, arm of supporting leg above head, other arm to side
1, — Lift forward leg *en l'air*
2, 3, — Carry to *attitude effacé,* changing arms
4, — *Relevé allongée*
&5, — *Pas de basque* back without passing weight, lowering raised arm to side, other arm forward, palms downwards,
6, — *Pirouette en dehors,* arms low
7, — *Plié sur le cou-de-pied* back, arm of working leg opening to the side

8	*Glissade en croisé* back to half-toe, lifting back arm to shoulder, other arm open to side
	Repeat twice on each side

14 : Adage No. 2 [16 bars of 3/4]

1, 2,	*Grand plié* in 1st position, arms opening outwards from low to the side
3, 4,	Rise, lowering arms
5, 6, 7,	Press up to half-toe, arms lifting forward and up
8,	*Tombé en effacé* forward, keeping arms high
1, 2,	Lift back leg en *arabesque effacé,* lowering arm of supporting leg forward to eye-level, other arm opening to the side
3,	Carry leg to *effacé* forward, forward arm lifting to above head
4,	*Relevé*
5,	*Pas de basque* forward, lowering raised arm to the side and forward, other arm remaining side
6, 7,	*Pirouette en dedans,* finish *sur le cou-de-pied* front
8	*Glissade croisé* forward to half-toe, both hands on hips
	Repeat twice each side

15 : Adage No. 3 [16 bars of 3/4 *sostenuto*]

1, 2,	*Grand plié* in 5th position *croisé,* arms opening to side
3, 4,	Rise, lowering arms
5, 6, 7,	Balance *sur le cou-de-pied* front, lifting arm of supporting leg to side, other arm in front
8,	*Tombé en effacé* forward
1, 2,	*Pirouette piqué en dehors,* arms low
3, 4,	Finish in high *écarté* back, arm of extended leg high, other arm open to side
5,	Drop *tombé croisé* forward, lowering high arm to forward position
6, 7,	*Coupé* under and *renversé en dehors*
8	Finish *croisé* forward 4th position, both arms to the same side as back leg
	Repeat twice on each side

16 : Temps liés [4 bars 2/4 *andantino grazioso*]

&1, &2,	*Temps lié croisé* forward
&3, &4,	*Temps lié croisé* back
&1, &2,	3 *Battements tendus* turning *en dehors* with back foot closing front, back, front
&3, &4	*Pirouette en dehors* from 5th position, closing 5th position front

Repeat on other side, and twice more

17 : Battements fondus [3 bars of 12/8 *molto moderato*]

1, &2, &	*Battement fondu effacé* front
3,	*Tombé en effacé* forward
&a4,	*Pas de bourrée* under
1, &a2,	*Battement fondu en effacé* back with back leg
3,	*Coupé* under
&a4,	*Pas de bourrée* under finishing 4th position *croisé*
1, &2,	*Pirouette en dehors sur le cou-de-pied*
3, &4,	Finishing *arabesque croisé*
&	*Coupé* under and repeat other side

Repeat sequence twice more on half-toe

18 : Ronds de jambe en l'air [4 bars 2/4 *allegretto leggiero*]

	Stand 5th position *croisé*, left foot front
	Travel diagonally
1,	*Coupé* under with back leg
&2,	*Rond de jambe sauté en dehors*, finishing *en l'air* to the side
3,	*Coupé* under
&4,	Small *cabriole ouvert en effacé devant*
1,	*Tombé en effacé* forward
&2,	Half turn *en dedans* and *cabriole en arabesque*, with back to audience
&	*Coupé* under with half turn, continuing same way
3,	*Tombé en effacé* forward
&4	*Pirouette en dedans* finishing 5th position front
	Continue in same direction

Repeat diagonally from other side

19 : Petits battements [4 bars of 2/4 *moderato ma giocoso*]

	Stand 5th position *croisé*
&1,	*Sissonne en tournant en dehors*, finishing 5th position front
&2,	Repeat *sissonne en tournant*
&3, &4,	3 *Petits battements*
&1,	*Sissonne tombé en effacé* forward
&2,	*Sissonne tombé en croisé* forward
&3,	*Cabriole failli* finishing 4th position *croisé*
&4	*Pirouette en dehors* finishing 5th position front

Repeat other side, and twice more

20 : Allegro No. 1 [1 bar 3/2 *moderato giocoso*]
Stand 5th position *croisé*

&1,	*Glissade devant*
&2,	*Petit jeté* with front leg, other leg finishing *sur le cou-de-pied* behind
&3,	*Glissade derrière*
&4,	*Petit jeté* with back leg, other leg finishing *sur le cou-de-pied* in front
&5,	*Jeté croisé en avant*
&6	*Assemblé* over

Repeat other side, and twice more

21 : Allegro No. 2 [1 bar 4/4, 1 bar 3/4, *poco allegretto*]
Stand 5th position *croisé*
Travel diagonally

&1,	*Glissade derrière*
&2,	*Entrechat cinq devant*
&3, &4,	2 *Chassés en croisé*
&1,	*Sissonne en tournant en dehors,* picking up back leg and finishing 4th position *effacé* forward
&2, &3	*Pirouette en dedans,* finishing 4th position *croisé* forward

Repeat in same direction

Repeat diagonally from other side

22 : Allegro No. 3 [4 bars of 6/8 *allegretto e legato*]
Stand 5th position *croisé*
Travel diagonally

&1,	*Glissade derrière*
&2,	*Ballonné en écarté* forward
&3,	*Ballonné passé* back
&4,	*Coupé* under and *tombé en croisé*
1,	*Pas de basque* back
&2, &3,	*Pirouette en dehors* finishing *attitude effacé*
&4	Brush working leg across to 4th position *croisé en avant*

Repeat in same direction

Repeat diagonally from other side

23 : Grands sauts [8 bars of 3/4 *allegro vigoroso*]
Begin down-stage *en arabesque effacé*

&a1,	*Pas de bourrée couru* turning diagonally upstage
&a2,	*Entrechat cinq en tournant* landing 5th position
&a3,	*Entrechat trois derrière*

&a4,	*Sissonne tombé en arrière croisé*
&a	*Coupé* under with half turn upstage
1, &a2,	Continuing turn *jeté en attitude croisé* down-stage *(coupé-jeté en tournant)*
&a3, &a4	*Passé* back leg through into *piqué en arabesque effacé*

Repeat other way, and twice more

24 : Grands sauts (for boys) [8 bars of 3/4 *valse molto vigoroso*]

Stand 4th position *croisé*

Travel diagonally

&1,	*Glissade derrière* from 4th position to 4th position
&a2,	*Entrechat cinq de volé*
&3, &4,	*Soutenu en dehors* (front leg opens side and gathers)
1,	*Demi-plié* 5th position
&2, &3,	2 *Entrechats six*
&4	*Pas de basque* forward

Repeat in same direction

Repeat from other side

In this *enchaînment, tour en l'air* may be substituted for 2 *entrechats six,* in which case the step will travel in alternate directions.

25 : Pointe work (for girls) Enchaînement 1 [2 bars 2/4 *moderato e legato*]

Stand 5th position *croisé*

&1,	*Glissade croisé en avant*
&2,	*Demi-plié* in 5th position
&3, &4,	Repeat *glissade* and *plié*
&1,	*Assemblé* over *en pointe*
&2,	*Demi-plié* in 5th position
&3, &4	2 *Échappés* to 2nd position with change of leg

Repeat on other side

Repeat twice in reverse

26 : Enchaînement 2 [4 bars 3/4 *valse lyrique*]

Stand 5th position *croisé*

&a	*Demi-plié* and *petit développé en effacé*
1,	*Piqué en arabesque effacé*
&a2,	Lower working leg through 1st position *demi-plié* to 4th position *croisé*
&a	*Petit développé* with back leg to *effacé* front
3,	*Piqué en arabesque effacé*
&a4	*Plié, relevé sur le cou-de-pied derrière* turning body to the *croisé* position

Repeat on other side, and twice more

27 : Batterie (for boys) [2 bars of 2/4 *polka moderato*]
Stand on forward leg, back leg pointed 4th position *croisé*
Travel diagonally

&1, *Brisé volé* forward
&2, *Brisé volé* back
&3, *Pas de basque* back (step side, back)
&4 *Pas de basque en tournant* with front leg *(en dedans)*

Repeat in same direction

Repeat diagonally from other side

28 : Glissades battu (Brisés from 4th position to 4th position) [2/4 *giocoso*]
Travel diagonally
Series of *glissades battu* from 4th position to 4th position, using alternate *épaulement*

Repeat from other side

29 : Pointe work (for girls) Enchaînement 3 [2 bars of 2/4 *galop*]
Travel diagonally
Stand 5th position *croisé*

1, 2, 2 *Emboîtés en pointe*
3, *Tombé en effacé en avant*
&4 *Petit jeté en tournant*

Repeat in series same direction

Repeat from other side

30 : Enchaînement 4 [2 bars of 2/4 *galop*]
Stand 5th position *croisé*
Travel diagonally

&1, *Piqué pirouette en dedans*
2, *Piqué pirouette en dehors* (stepping from *pointe* to *pointe)*
& *Demi-plié sur le cou-de-pied*
3, *Relevé ballonné en écarté*
4 *Demi-plié sur le cou-de-pied*

Repeat in series same direction

Repeat from other side

31 : Batterie (for boys and girls) [1 bar 3/4 *alla polacca, un poco cantabile*]

	Stand 5th position *croisé*
&1,	*Entrechat trois derrière*
&	*Coupé* under
2,	*Jeté battu derrière*
&3	*Brisé en avant*

Repeat on other side, and twice more

32 : Variation of battements tendus and grands battements

Révérence

Note: The time signatures, indications of tempo and counts are recommended by Barbara Gregory.

Class remembered by Cleo Nordi

Class VII

BARRE-WORK

1 : Grands pliés [3/4 *valse lento*]

Preparation: stand in 5th position, *tendu* front leg to 2nd position, follow by *tendu* with other leg (half length) to 2nd position

&1, &2,	*Plié* in 2nd position
&3, &4,	Rise to flat foot
&1, &2,	*Relevé* to *demi-pointe* and hold balance, arms above head
&3, &4,	Lower heels and *tendu* to 1st position
&1, &2,	*Plié* in 1st position
&3, &4,	Rise
&1, &2,	*Relevé* to *demi-pointe* and balance, arms above head
&3, &4	Lower heels and *tendu* to 5th position

Repeat sequence 5th position front and 5th position back

Soutenu en tournant (détourné) and repeat whole sequence on other side

2 : Battements tendus [2/4 *moderato*]

&1, &2 — 2 *Battements tendus devant,* 1 *simple,* 1 with *plié* in 5th position

Repeat to the side finishing back

Repeat to the back

Repeat to the side finishing front

Repeat whole sequence

Repeat to the side in 1st position

3 : Battements tendus jetés [2/4 *allegro*]

&1, &2, &3,	3 *Battements tendus jetés, devant, de côté, derrière*
&4	1 *Battement tendu jeté devant* with change of leg

Repeat in reverse

Repeat sequence 8 times

4 : Battements fondus [3/4 *lento*]

1, &a2, *Battement fondu en face devant* rising to *demi-pointe*
&a3, *Tombé en avant* into *arabesque en plié*
&a4 Return to supporting leg with working leg extended *devant*
Repeat movement to the side, holding extension *à la seconde en plié*

Repeat movement to the back, holding extension *devant en plié*

Repeat movement again to the side

Hold balance in the *tire-bouchon* position, arms above head

5 : Battements frappés [2/4 *vivo*]

Commence from *sur le cou-de-pied* front
&1, &2, 2 *Battements frappés de côté*
&3, *Tombé devant*
&4, *Coupé dessous,* opening *à la seconde*
&1, &2, &3, &4 4 *Battements frappés de côté*

Repeat sequence in reverse

Repeat whole movement on *demi-pointe*

Hold balance *à la seconde* on *demi-pointe*

6 : Ronds de jambe par terre [3/4 *polonaise*]

1, 2, 3, *Piqué devant, de côté, derrière*
1, 2, 3 *Ronds de jambe en dehors*
3 Close 5th position *derrière*

Repeat *en dedans*

Repeat again *en dehors* and *en dedans*

7 : Simple port de bras in 5th position [*valse molto cantabile*]

Arm open to the side, bend forward, arm following down, raise body, lifting arm to above head, bend backwards, opening arm to side

Repeat *port de bras* on *demi-pointe*

8 : Ronds de jambe en l'air [3/4 *moderato con moto*]

&1, &2,	2 *Ronds de jambe en l'air en dehors*
&3, &4,	*Passé,* and extend working leg to *effacé devant en plié*
&1, &2, &3,	Brush leg through 1st position to *attitude effacé derrière,* straightening supporting leg
&4	Close 5th position *derrière*
	Repeat in reverse
	Repeat sequence *en dehors* and *en dedans* on *demi-pointe*
	Hold balance *en attitude effacé devant*

9 : Adagio [3/4 *valse lyrique*]

	Commence from 5th position
&a1, &a2,	*Fouetté en dehors*
&a3,	Finish in *développé devant*
&a4,	Open leg to *à la seconde*
&a1,	*Passé*
&a2, &a3,	Extend leg to *arabesque allongée,* with both arms forward, and balance
&a4,	Close 5th position *derrière*
&a1, &a2,	*Fouetté en dedans*
&a3,	Finishing *en arabesque*
&a4,	Open leg to *à la seconde*
&a1,	*Passé*
&a2,	*Développé en avant*
&a3, &a4	Hold balance with arms above head
	Repeat on *demi-pointe*

10 : Grands battements [2/4 *alla marcia*]

	Commence from 5th position
&a1, &a2 for each *grand battement*	4 *Grands battements en croix* rising to *demi-pointe,* and finishing 5th position *demi-plié*
	4 *Grands battements en croix* rising to *demi-pointe,* and closing 5th position without *plié*
	Repeat sequence again

11 : Petits battements [2/4 *vivo*]

	Preparation *tendu* to 2nd position and bring foot to *sur le cou-de-pied devant*
1 to 5,	5 *Petits battements* with accent *devant sur le cou-de-pied,* finishing *en plié*
6,	Hold *demi-plié*

7, 8	Straighten supporting leg

Repeat sequence with accent *sur le cou-de-pied derrière*

Repeat sequence

Hold balance *sur le cou-de-pied,* arms low

12 : Pointes at the barre (facing barre) [2/4 allegro]

1, &2,	*Échappé à la seconde*
3, &4,	*Demi-plié à la seconde* and *entrechat six sauté* to 5th position
1 to 4,	Repeat
1 to 8	4 *Échappés changés*

Repeat 4 times

Hold balance 2nd position *en pointe,* arms above head

CENTER-WORK

13 : Adage No. 1 [24 bars of 3/4 *andante*]

1, 2,	*Grand plié* in 2nd position
3, 4,	Quick rise to *arabesque effacé, en diagonal*
1, 2, 3,	*Passé croisé en avant*
4,	*Tombé* 4th position to knee
5, 6, 7,	Quick *relevé en attitude croisé,* and hold
8,	*Plié en attitude croisé*
1, 2,	*Coupé dessous,* and *pas de basque en avant* to 4th position *croisé*
3, 4,	*Pirouette en dehors*
1, 2,	Finish 4th position *en plié, pointe tendu derrière*
3, 4	Change position to *pointe tendu devant,* arms open to the side

Repeat twice on each side

14 : Adage No. 2 [24 bars of 4/4 *maestoso*]

1, 2,	*Grand plié* in 1st position *en face*
3, 4,	Quick *relevé* with *développé à la seconde*
1, 2, 3, 4,	*Passé* and extend into *arabesque croisé*
1, 2,	*Plié* in 4th position *croisé*
3, 4,	*Relevé à la seconde*
1, 2, 3, 4,	*Promenade à la seconde en dedans*
1, 2, 3,	*Passé and développé croisé en avant*
4,	*Tombé* 4th position *croisé,* lift back leg

1, 2,	*Fouetté en dedans*
3, 4	Finish 5th position *devant, soussus,* arms *écarté*
	Repeat twice on each side

15 : Adage No. 3 [3/4 or 6/8 *andantino*]

1, 2,	*Grand plié* in 5th position *croisé*
3, 4,	Rise
1, 2, 3, 4,	*Relevé sur le cou-de-pied devant,* front arm forward, other arm open to side,
1, 2, 3, 4,	*Développé croisé en avant*
1,	*Tombé croisé en avant*
2,	*Sissonne tombé effacé en avant,* same direction
3, 4,	*Fouetté en dedans,* arms above head
1,	Close 5th position *devant, en plié*
2, 3, 4	*Grand sissonne failli* to the knee, arms back in *allongée*
	Repeat twice on each side

16 : Temps liés [3/4 *allegretto e cantabile*]

	Stand 5th position *croisé*
&1,	*Tombé effacé en avant*
&2,	*Piqué pirouette en dehors*
&3,	*Tombé effacé en avant,* continuing same direction
&4,	*Fouetté en dedans,* close 5th position *devant*
&1, &2,	*Temps lié croisé en avant*
&3, &4	*Temps lié croisé en arrière*
	Repeat on other side, and twice more

17 : Battements tendus [2/4 *allegretto giocoso*]

	Stand 5th position *en face*
&1, &2,	3 *Battements tendus simple, devant, de côté, derrière*
&3,	Quick *glissade écarté en avant*
&4	Quick *glissade écarté en arrière*
	Repeat on other side, and twice more

18 : Battements fondus [3/4 *allegretto con moto*]

	Preparation 4th position *croisé, pointe tendu derrière*
&1,	*Coupé dessous*
&2,	*Battement fondu à la seconde* to *demi-pointe*
&3,	Hold *demi-pointe*

&4	*Passé* into *arabesque croisé en plié*
	Repeat other side, and twice more

19 : Battements frappés [6/8 *allegro*]

	Preparation: stand *en face, pointe tendu à la seconde*
&1, &2,	3 *Battements frappés de côté,* third finished in *plié*
&3, &4,	*Jeté de côté* with *passé en avant croisé en plié*
1, &2,	*Fouetté en dehors*
&3,	Finish *tombé en effacé* to *arabesque allongée,* both arms forward
&4	Close 5th position
	Repeat on other side, and twice more

20 : Ronds de jambe en l'air [3/8 *allegro moderato*]

	Commence in 5th position
1, &2,	2 *Ronds de jambe en l'air en dehors*
3, &4,	2 *Ronds de jambe en l'air en dedans*
&1,	*Passé* and extend working leg *croisé en avant*
2,	*Fouetté en dehors*
3,	Finish *tombé à la seconde*
4	Close 5th position *soussus,* hands on hips
	Repeat on other side, and twice more

21 : Petits battements [2/4 *galop*]

	Commence 4th position *croisé, pointe tendu devant*
	Travel diagonally
&1, &2,	3 *Chaînés*
&3, &4,	*Jeté de côté* bringing working leg to *sur le cou-de-pied devant*
&1, &2,	*Relevé en tournant en dedans* with 3 *petits battements*
&3, &4	*Coupé dessous en plié*
	Repeat in same direction
	Repeat from other side

22 : Allegro No. 1 [3/4 *valse allegro*]

	Commence 5th position *croisé*
&1,	*Assemblé dessus*
&2,	2 *Changements de pieds*
&3,	*Assemblé dessous*
&4	*Failli*

Repeat on other side, and twice more

23 : Allegro No. 2 [3/8 *allegro vivo*]

	Commence 4th position *croisé, pointe tendu devant*
&a1,	*Glissade derrière*
&a2,	*Jeté battu sur le cou-de-pied*
&a3,	*Coupé dessous* and *pas de basque en avant*
&a4	*Coupé dessous* and *ballonné battu derrière, en tournant en dedans*

Repeat on other side, and twice more

24 : Allegro No. 3 [6/8 *allegro moderato*]

	Commence 4th position, *pointe tendu derrière*
1, &2,	*Ballotté effacé en avant*
3, &4,	*Ballotté effacé en arrière*
1, &2,	*Failli*
3, &4	*Pirouette en dehors,* finish *en plié sur le cou-de-pied derrière*

Repeat on other side, and twice more

25 : Pointe-work (for girls) [2/4 *moderato con moto*]

	Stand 5th position *croisé*
&1,	*Assemblé dessus*
&2,	*Relevé derrière, plié* 5th position
&3,	*Relevé devant, plié* 5th position
&4	*Relevé derrière, plié* 5th position

Repeat on other side, and twice more

26 : Pointe-work [4/4 *moderato cantabile*]

	Stand 4th position *croisé, pointe tendu devant*
&1, &2,	*Pas de bourrée effacé en avant*
&3, &4,	*Coupé dessous* and *piqué pirouette en dedans*
&1, &2,	*Tombé croisé en avant*
&3, &4	*Bourrée écarté en arrière*

Repeat on other side, and twice more

27 : Grands sauts (for boys) [3/4 *valse moderato*]

	Commence 4th position, *pointe tendu derrière*
&a1,	*Pas de bourrée couru effacé en avant*
&a2,	*Grand jeté en attitude croisé*

&a3,	*Coupé dessous* and *pas de basque en avant*
&a4,	*Grand entrechat cinq de volé*
&1, &2, &3,	3 *Sissonnes fermés écartés en arrière*
&4	[illegible]
	Repeat other side, and twice more

28 : Pointe-work (for girls) [3/4 *valse vivo*]

	Commence 5th position *croisé*
&	*Petit sissonne sauté sur le cou-de-pied devant*
1, &2,	*Piqué en attitude effacé*
&3,	*Plié* and *relevé passé croisé en avant,* arms above head
&4	Close 5th position and *soussus,* arms open to the side
	Repeat on other side, and twice more

29 : Pointe-work [2/4 *allegro*]

	Commence 5th position *en face*
&1,	*Échappé,* remaining on *pointe*
&2,	Bring forward leg to *sur le cou-de-pied devant en plié*
&3,	*Fouetté en dehors*
&4	Close 5th position *derrière*
	Repeat other side, and twice more

30 : Batterie (for boys) [3/4 *vivo alla mazurka*]

	Commence 4th position *croisé, pointe tendu derrière*
&1,	*Brisé volé en avant sur le cou-de-pied devant*
&2,	*Échappé* to 2nd position
&3	*Entrechat trois derrière*
	Repeat on other side, and twice more

31 : Circular manège (for girls) [2/4 *galop*]

	Commence 4th position *croisé, pointe tendu devant*
16 bars	*Chaîné* round the studio
	Finish *piqué* and drop to 4th position
	Repeat on other side

32 : Grands battements [4/4 *alla marcia*]

	Stand 5th position *en face*
1, &2,	*Tombé en effacé en avant*
3, &4,	*Piqué pirouette en dehors,* closing 5th position *derrière*
1, 2, 3, 4	2 *Grands battements de côté* advancing forwards

Repeat 4 times forward

Repeat 4 times in reverse

Révérence

PART III

APPENDIXES

THE PIROUETTE

1. Fifth Position. Préparation pour la pirouette en dehors sur le cou-de-pied.
2. Préparation pour la pirouette sur le cou-de-pied en dehors.
3. Second Position. Préparation pour la pirouette en dehors.
4. Fourth Position (effacé). Préparation pour la pirouette en dedans sur le cou-de-pied.
5. Fourth Position (croisé). Préparation pour la pirouette en dedans sur le cou-de-pied.

Drawings by Nicolas Legat to illustrate the theories of preparation for pirouettes. Originally published in the Dancing Times, *September 1936.*

Appendix 1: The Secret of the Pirouette

Extracts from notes of Nicolas Legat and André Eglevsky

THERE ARE MANY ASPECTS TO CONSIDER in diagnosing the essential elements that contribute to the harmonious execution of a *pirouette* or a series of turns.

The *pirouette* is a feat of artistic acrobatics involving a delicate adjustment of equilibrium and rotating movement. It consists of a rapid spinning of the vertical body on the half-point or point of the toe.

The three essential elements for turning with technical proficiency are vision, power and balance.

The eyes provide vision. For turning it is necessary to spot. This means focusing the eyes, not upon a specific object, but straight ahead beyond the wall or mirror or spotlight in front of you. As the body turns the head remains facing front until the last moment, then it is brought quickly round in advance of the body. In other words, the head and eyes are the last to leave the spot as the body turns, and the first to return to it.

The power, or momentum, for *pirouetting* comes from the impetus set in motion by the coordinated impulse of the arms and shoulders together with the *relevé,* or push-up, from the floor. Academically the arms should be rounded, forming arcs from the shoulders, the finger-tips not quite meeting in front of the body. Men may obtain more power and speed by commencing a series of turns with the arms wide open to the side, and gradually closing the arms forward and round in front of the body. Such a motion aids acceleration and facilitates spin.

The facility for performing a quantity of turns calls for impeccable balance. In the preparation from fourth position, the weight of the body should be entirely over the forward leg (see illustration); thus no adjustment is necessary when rising on to it. It will be noted that this is a distinctly different practice from other systems where, in the preparation, the weight of the body is equally distributed between the two legs.

The body is not absolutely vertical during a *pirouette,* but inclines very slightly forward. The adjustment which keeps the body from swaying or falling off the *pirouette* is in the back. The shoulders are pressed down with the shoulderblades flat, the dorsal muscles held firmly, and the buttocks gripped tightly. Throughout the turn the muscles of the supporting knee are forcibly contracted, while a feeling of elongation or growing-up from the hips is maintained. A lightness resides in the body, which is the dominating spirit of the *pirouette.*

Where a series of *pirouettes* is attempted, the force of gravity is counteracted by subtle turning in the hip muscles. A gripping of the hip of the lifted leg was advocated by Legat, but this is a manipulation that should not be exaggerated, or even attempted, until the dancer has mastered the basic fundamentals.

Technically the *pirouette* expresses some degree of perfection when the body, gradually exhausting the spin like a top, comes to a standstill in the *pirouetting* pose. In practice one should aim at attaining this skill, and the mastery of effortless finishing. The finish of a *pirouette* is undoubtedly one of the most important features; the final pose is the last impression left in the spectator's eye, and many an imperfect *pirouette* may be salvaged by an effective finish. For stage effect, the finish of a *pirouette* is embellished by springing into an attractive pose, which should be bold and self-confident, but without arrogance. Artistry without vanity.

Appendix 2: Class Music

Composed by Nicolas Legat, arranged by Vladimir Launitz

IN THE MARYINSKY DAYS when Legat was professor of the Class of Perfection, he accompanied his class on the violin. In later years, he conducted his class seated at the piano and from there provided all the rhythmic subtleties and nuances that gave emphasis and highlights to his lessons. And, more than this, he brought his vivacious wit to the keyboard, and with a trill, a *glissando* or a discord he would underline the dancers' mistakes.

Legat always improvised his music, as he did his dance *enchaînements*. Unfortunately, his individual style and the quality of his playing were never recorded. However, his friend and collaborator, Vladimir Launitz, wrote down a number of Legat's improvisations, and arranged them for the class accompaniment.

These tunes are period pieces, and, as such, give a flavor of the classroom, but little else. Such simple, flowing, sentimental rhythms might be termed good "muscle" music, but it is difficult to convey the way Legat himself played it. He was inimitable. Not only did he use conventional, square rhythms, but many broken rhythms which so well suited his light, quick *allegro*. He established the mood of the class with dynamic and extended *rubato*, not to mention the long drawn-out *tremolos* that accompanied the unending *pirouettes* of André Eglevsky.

The music is included here, not as a recommended accompaniment for class, but rather as an album of something remembered, to be brought out on occasion and savored for its flow and buoyancy, and, perhaps, to be studied by aspiring ballet accompanists. The exercises included with the music are not those used by Legat; they were added by an editor after Legat's death.

Vladimir Launitz drawn by Legat.

PART I.

EXERCISES AT THE BAR.

(Explanatory Notes and Music by NICOLAS LEGAT.)

1st EXERCISE: Pliés, and half toe. Twice in the 2nd position and twice in the 1st position; in the 5th position twice with right foot in front, and twice with left foot in front.

Tempo di Valse lente. M.M. ♩= 88

2nd EXERCISE: Battements tendus demi-pliés.

Allegretto. M.M. ♩= 108

N.L. 100

3rd EXERCISE: Battements tendus simples.

Sostenuto. M.M. ♪ = 96

4 th EXERCISE: Battements tendus jetés.

Allegretto non troppo. M.M. ♩ = 84.

N.L.100

9th EXERCISE: Developés.

Lento. M.M. ♩= 63

10th EXERCISE: Grands battements jetés.

A la marcia. M.M. ♩= 116

11th EXERCISE: Petits battements sur le cou-de-pied.

A la marcia. M.M. ♩= 144.

N.L.100

PART II.
EXERCISES IN THE CENTRE.

(Explanatory Notes and Music by NICOLAS LEGAT.)

1st. EXERCISE: Pliés, and half toe. Twice in the 2nd. position and twice in the 1st. position; in the 5th. position twice with right foot in front, and twice with left foot in front

Tempo di Valse lente M.M. ♩ = 80

2nd. EXERCISE: Temps lié. Demi-plié, glissé croisé en avant with R. closing 5th. in demi-plié; continue same de côté, then repeat with L.

Tempo di Valse lente M.M. ♩ = 132

3rd. EXERCISE: Battements tendus.
Allegretto non troppo M.M. 𝅗𝅥 = 92.

4th. EXERCISE: Battements fondus.
Andantino ♩ = 102.

5th. EXERCISE: Battements frappés.
Allegretto M.M. ♩ = 74.

6th. EXERCISE: Rond de jambes en dehors en l'air.
Moderato M.M. ♩ = 63.

7th. EXERCISE: Rond de jambes en dedans en l'air. (Use music for ex.6)
Moderato M.M. ♩ = 63.

7ª ADDITIONAL EXERCISE: After rond de jambes en dedans en l'air, attitude effaceé passing into croisé (same leg).
Adagio rubato M.M. ♩ = 60.

8th. EXERCISE: Grand battements jetés.
A la Marcia M.M. 𝅗𝅥 = 76.

9th. EXERCISE: Petits battements sur le cou de-pied.
Allegro non troppo M.M. ♩ = 146.

10 th. EXERCISE: Plié 5th.pos.half toes, developé à la second, passer la jambe and arabesque croisé.

Adagio M.M.♩ = 60.

10ª EXERCISE: Plié 5th. pos. developé to croisé en avant, demi-plié, step forward on to R. developé effacé en avant with L, passer la jambe and arabesque.

Adagio M.M.♩ = 60.

11 th. EXERCISE: Assemblé, two petits changements de pieds.

Allegretto non troppo M.M.♩ = 108.

12th. EXERCISE: 2 jetés and assemblé, pause, (4 times)
Con forza M.M. ♩ = 174.

13th. EXERCISE: Glissade, balloné, pas de basque, and jeté, (4 times)
Allegretto leggiere M.M. ♩ = 64.

Legat in Harlequinade.

MINDY ALOFF is the editor of the writings of Agnes de Mille, *Leaps in the Dark: Art and the World,* and served as editor of *Dance in America: A Reader's Anthology.*

TASHA BERTRAM, the British dancer, actress, songwriter, choreographer, and teacher of ballet, studied at the Legat School from 1970 to 1978. She spent most of her professional career dancing with London City Ballet, the touring company that flourished from 1978 to 1996 and for which Diana, Princess of Wales, served as patron. Later on, Bertram formed her own family band, Winnet, writing all her own songs (lyrics and music), and staging its presentations. She now works internationally as a freelance ballet teacher in the Legat system and serves as an examiner with the Russian Ballet Society.

ROBERT GRESKOVIC has been writing about dance since 1973. He reviews dance for the *Wall Street Journal.* He is the author of *Ballet 101: The Complete Guide to Learning and Loving the Ballet* and has served as consulting editor for *Baryshnikov: In Black and White* and consultant for *Ballet* by Kate Castle. Greskovic has taught dance history and aesthetics at Princeton University, Sarah Lawrence College, The City College of New York, and Hunter College. His dance reviews and feature stories have appeared in the *Village Voice*, the *Los Angeles Times*, the *New York Times*, and other publications. His personal collection of historical dance items includes numerous Imperial Ballet photocards as well as over thirty individual plates from *The Russian Ballet in Caricature* by the Legat brothers.